COME SKI WITH ME

COME SKI WITH ME

By Stein Eriksen

Edited by Martin Luray

WITH PHOTOGRAPHS BY FRED LINDHOLM

BONANZA BOOKS · NEW YORK

ACKNOWLEDGMENTS

To Ziff-Davis Publishing Company
for permission to use text material
and photographs that have
previously appeared in *Skiing*
magazine. To Universal Publishing
and Distributing Corporation
for permission to excerpt from articles
that have appeared in *Ski* magazine
and for the use of photographs and
photographic sequences that appeared
in *Ski*. To Jakob Vaage of the
Norwegian Ski Museum, Oslo, for his
invaluable help in preparing the
source material for the chapter
entitled "A Short History of Skiing."

DESIGNED BY LAWRENCE FABER

FOR
My father and mother,
Marius and Birgit Eriksen,
and my brother,
Marius, Jr., who
instilled in me a love
for skiing, and for
Kjell Borge Andersen
who gave so much
of himself to make it
possible for me to further the
cause of Norwegian racing.

CONTENTS

PHOTO SOURCES

All photos in "A Short History of Skiing" courtesy Jakob Vaage. 40, A. Bauman, Wengen, Jul. Burch, Wengen; 41, Jul. Burch, Wengen; 45, Jakob Vaage; 47 UPI Photo; 49, (bottom) Knut Skarland; 50, ViMenn; 57, Sun Valley News Bureau; 59, Gunnar Larsson.
Color section, black and white portfolios, end papers, instructional photos, Fred Lindholm.

To me, gracefulness on skis
should be the end-all
of the sport...

In the days when I was involved with skiing for fun, but not yet with ski journalism, Stein Eriksen, like his Norse ancestors, seemed more myth than reality. To most of us he typified a phenomenal ability on skis. He had a kind of alchemy that mixed great physical and acrobatic prowess with elán. What one saw in Stein was something magical; combined with that confident verve and those unbelievable reverse shoulder turns was a genuine love for the mountains and for the snow. Sheer happiness always shone through. There were the mountains, and the traces of powder, and there was Stein incredibly floating on his edges—his body curved into the outrigger-like position that has come to be known as the Stein turn.

As the editor of *Ski* magazine and later of *Skiing,* I began working with him on a series of instructional articles that had one basic premise—they were to be easy to understand and would concentrate on certain essential keys to the maneuvers. Understanding those keys and performing them correctly would lead to successful completion of the entire maneuver, whether it was something simple like the stem christie or more complicated, like jump wedeln. Much of that material has been incorporated in this book and in fact, the idea for the book was a result of happy reader reaction to the articles.

After a half-decade of collaborating with Stein, I know that while the public myth of a skiing god still surrounds him, he is privately a hard-working, complete professional —strong on technique and the knowledge of how to transmit its details. He has been

FOREWORD

exacting in the preparation of this book, just as he is exacting in the administration of his ski school at Sugarbush Valley and his other activities.

Stein Eriksen is perhaps the embodiment of Otto Schniebs' often-quoted dictum about skiing being "a way of life." In a sense he was bred to skiing; the younger son in a family preoccupied with the sport. His father, a gymnast and cross-country skier, who saw alpine skiing as the sport's future, was the inventor and manufacturer of the first modern alpine ski. His brother, a Norwegian slalom champion, is a national hero, a veteran of the RAF who survived two years in a German prison camp after downing 12 Nazi planes. His mother organized Oslo's first women's ski club. Now in her late sixties, she still skis.

Stein's youth was a golden one. There were few conflicts—only the challenges that came with mastering first the art of skiing, then the art of racing. His accomplishments—gold and silver medals in the 1952 Olympic Winter Games and two gold medals in the 1954 World Ski Championships (FIS)—have been surpassed only by Toni Sailer. But only Stein has been able to parlay what he knows about skiing into an immensely successful career.

All of this knowledge is imparted on the following pages. The reader cannot but discover, as I did in editing the book that in skiing, one is constantly learning something new. And that, as much as anything else, is Stein's secret.

MARTIN LURAY

MY SKIING HERITAGE

1

To understand why I ski, it is necessary to go back to my childhood. The things we do and the decisions we make in our adult life often reflect the kind of childhood we have had. Mine was one of happiness and understanding mixed with love.

I grew up in a skiing household. I remember skiing cross-country behind our house and as I made tracks in the snow I would scare up rabbits and foxes. Once in a while a bird would take off beside me as I skied. These were my first experiences on skis—an early feeling of oneness with nature.

My mittens and sweater were always covered with snow, and when I returned home there would always be a warm welcome from my mother and father. The wet clothes would be put to dry on a heater in the hall and the mittens and socks hung up on nails above it. Exhausted, I would tumble into bed and dream about all I had seen and done during the day. I could wish for no other life—and this is why I ski.

Then, during my early racing years, there was always encouragement from my

INTRODUCTION

WHY I SKI

father. He had a gentle way of teaching the difference between a good and bad sportsman. There was his overwhelming joy at my victories and the kind understanding of the losses. Then came years of hard training and racing with all of the friendships that I was able to make through skiing.

And now there is another great reward in being able to give some of these experiences to many people who have never known such a way of life. My great joy is in teaching them confidence and seeing their love for the sport increase every day that they put on skis.

That is why I ski.

Norwegians have known about this way of life for a thousand years. Long before skis were used for sliding downhill or across the countryside they were a means of survival for my ancestors. "They are a nation on skis," a visitor to Norway once wrote. To learn more about the sport, it might be useful to go back to the beginning.

A SHORT HISTORY OF SKIING
Back to the Great God Nor

ACCORDING TO ANCIENT LEGEND, the god Nor is the ancestor of all Norwegians. When he first reached the Norwegian border, so the story goes, he was stopped by a violent blizzard. He put on skis, continued his journey, and took possession of the land that is now Norway. Thus the first time the name "Norway" is mentioned in legend, skis are too. In the Norse pantheon, other gods used skis: Ull is the god of skiing, and Skade the ski goddess.

This, of course, is legend. Closer to fact, it is known that some sort of skis were used by the prehistoric inhabitants of an area of Norway south of the Arctic Circle. A rock-carving found near Rødøy shows a man on skis; archaeologists say the carving was made some 4000 years ago. Other rock carvings found in Russia prove the archaeologists' contention. Remnants of skis have been found in peat bogs in Norway, Finland, Sweden, and Russia. The oldest of these "bog" skis found in Finland and Sweden date back about 4500 years.

Here are some actual dates in the history of skiing:

900 A. D.

Snorre, writer of sagas, described the Norwegian Vikings as "good skiers." They achieved feats on skis that were recounted through the centuries.

960

Skiing was mentioned as a necessary attribute of high-born warriors. Both kings and chiefs were practiced in skiing.

995–1026

King Olav Trygveson was described as a skier who was better at the sport than most other men. A famous archer, Arnljot Gelline, is said to have carried two compatriots on his skis when he was pursued by the enemy, and still he skied "as fast as if he were alone."

1030

King Harald Haardraade wrote a poem about eight achievements he had mastered. One of the achievements was skiing.

1120

The chronicles told of the dispute between two royal brothers, Sigurd and Öistein. Like après-skiers of today, Öistein was reported to have

Ancient ski, above,
was found in
a swamp in southern
Norway. Carbon dating
proved it to be about
2500 years old.
"Birch-leg" soldiers,
below, carry a Norwegian
king to safety, circa 1200.
Legend has it that they
smuggled him on skis
from Gudbrandsdal
to Trondheim. From a
painting by Knud Larsen
Bergslien in the Norwegian
Ski Museum at Holmenkollen.

Idealized in this painting is North Pole explorer Fridtjof Nansen. He holds a game bird. Note the fur boots and single pole.

Two skiers, left, circa 1889, hold skis with oldest known patented bindings— birch roots twisted into shape to hold boot heels in place. Above, in white, Karl Tellefsen, founder of the first American ski club.

16

told his brother, "I can manage the skis better than you can."

1200

In the winter of 1200, King Sverre used spies on skis in the civil war in Norway. But six years later war still ravaged Norway. King Sverre was dead. The two-year-old King Haakon Haakonson was saved from falling into enemy hands by the quick action of two skiers, who carried the infant king across the mountains from Gudbrandsdal to Österdal and then to Trondheim.

The epic is commemorated to this day by a marathon ski race that takes place along part of the same route used 750 years ago to save the infant king. The king's adherents in those days were called "birch legs," because their boots were made of birch bark when they were forced to live as outlaws. In their honor, the commemorative race is called "the birch-leg race." It covers a distance of thirty-five miles across the mountains. Up to a thousand cross-country skiers have competed each year since 1932.

1200–1700—Skis and skiing are mentioned only occasionally in Norwegian literature; however, skis were used by the Norwegian people to hunt and to move from one village to another; skis became part of Norwegian daily life.

1274

A code of law was made public in which it was forbidden for men on skis to pursue elk. The elk were at a disadvantage for they floundered in the snow and it was easy to catch them on skis. In *The King's Mirror*, written about this time, it was mentioned, "As soon as a man binds long pieces of wood to the feet he conquers the birds in their flight, the swiftest running dogs, or reindeer that are running with a speed twice as fast as regular deer. Then there are a lot of men who use skis so well that they can hit nine reindeer with their spears."

1535

Skiing was again mentioned in connection with hunting: ". . . to save the animals from the skiers" aspirations . . ." About this time, mail was delivered on skis. A report told of "lonely farmers who are glad when they hear the distant sound of the post horn and the mailman arrives on skis with messages from relatives or friends."

1550

A Swedish bishop wrote a book telling of his travels in Norway. It was published in Italy, and for the first time the Norwegian ability to travel on skis became known in Europe.

1713

The first ski troops were organized in Norway—companies of skiing soldiers. The interest in skiing increased rapidly.

1733

The first ski instruction book in Norway was written in German by Captain Jens Henrik Emmahusen of Trondheim.

1767

The first military ski competitions were held in Norway. Money was given as the award; the soldiers supplied their own skis, which they made themselves on their farms.

1808

During a war between Norway and Sweden, with Denmark allied with the Norwegians, ski soldiers played a large part in the proceedings. Skiing as a sport in Norway is considered to have begun with these skiing soldiers.

1850—MODERN SKIING BEGINS

The sport really began to take hold in the 19th century. By the end of the 19th century skiing had spread from its birthplace in Norway to all of the alpine countries of Europe and to the United States. The greatest single spur to skiing in Europe was a book by the polar explorer Fridtjof Nansen, *Crossing Greenland on Skis,* published in 1890 in three languages. "Skiing," Nansen wrote, "is a royal sport." His book took what had been Norwegian property and made it public knowledge.

Modern skiing actually began with the invention of a method of holding the heel in place. The inventor was a farmer's son named Sondre Norheim who lived in Morgedal in Telemark, Norway.

Up to that time, skis were being used in Norway, Sweden, Finland, Russia, and to some extent in Poland. About 1850, Norwegian immigrants began bringing skis into the United States, Australia, and Germany. Their primitive bindings consisted of a leather strap around the heel. It was loose and gave no support for the foot. Therefore it was nearly impossible to turn the skis or jump more than a few yards.

Sondre Norheim, a courageous young skier, decided that in order to take full advantage of his skis, he must be tied to them firmly as though they were ice skates. Norheim took thin birch roots, soaked them in hot water so that they would be flexible, and twisted them together so that they would fit around his heel and hold it in place.

In 1850, Norheim jumped sixty feet and a contemporary writer noted, "He stood on his skis down the steepest valley inclines and on mountainsides with the maximum of stability. He made graceful turns around bushes and trees, and was really an artist on skis."

Sondre Norheim was the father of ski jumping and of slalom. He was the first to execute a telemark turn and the first to do a Christiania[1]—this was more than a hundred years ago.

---

[1] The term "Christiania" was not used officially until 1901. What Norheim actually did was known as a "parallel telemark." In 1901 the "Central Association for Sports in Kristiania" wrote a basic rule book for jumping. It included a section on the types of turns used by the jumper to stop during the outrun. By mistake, the parallel stop turn, which had been used for fifty years in Telemark was referred to as a "Christiania." It was named for the capital of Norway, now Oslo.

*Norway's royal family
out for a Sunday
cross-country stroll.
Leading is the former
crown prince, now
King Olav, followed by
his mother, Queen Maude,
and father, King Haakon.
Photo taken in 1907.*

*Party of leading
Norwegian ski person-
alities in 1883.
The center figure
(in white) is Hjalmar
Welhaven, originator
of the Norwegian
Ski Museum.*

With the Norheim binding, plus the competitive spirit of the Norwegians, the sport began to move. The first ski races were held in Tromsö in 1843 and in Trysil in 1855. The first real ski jumping competition was held in Morgedal in 1866, and the hero of the day was Norheim. A journalist wrote, "with tucked-up legs he flew through the air like a bird."

From Telemark, deep in Norway, skiing spread to other mountains of the world. Norwegians emigrated to the United States and skiing came to America with them—particularly to the midwest and California.

1841—THE FIRST SKIERS IN THE UNITED STATES
The first men known to put skis into use in the United States were the immigrants Gullik Knudsen and brothers Ole and Ansten Nattestad from Numedal in Norway. In 1837 they had skied all the way from their home in the east of the country to the west coast of Norway to reach the ship that was to carry them to America. They settled in Illinois and it is known that they used skis on the Rock Prairie at Beloit near Chicago in 1841.

1852
Eivind Eielson, another Morgedal man, used skis in Dane County, Wisconsin, and later in Chaseburgh County in the same state.

1855
"Over 100 deer have been killed here by Norwegians because the poor animals cannot escape the hunters on skis," wrote a Norwegian settler to his family in Norway from Waupace Parsonage, Wisconsin.

Marius Eriksen, Stein's father, performs an elegant telemark turn. Picture was made in 1907.

1856

Soon after their arrival in America, Knudsen and the Nattestads wrote to a farm family in Tinn, Telemark, where they had stayed on their way across Norway. Inspired by the letter, the Thorensen family emigrated in 1838 and settled in the Midwest. The youngest of them, John, joined the gold rush to California in 1851. In the fall of 1855 he was the only applicant for the job of carrying the mail over Sierra Nevada. On January 3, 1856, John Thorensen departed on skis (they were called Norwegian snowshoes in contrast to the usual Indian webbed snowshoes) from Placerville, California, to carry the mail to Genoa in Carson Valley, Nevada. He was soon famous and was given the name "Snowshoe Thompson." His cross-Sierra trips for nearly 20 years made it possible for the mail to travel from San Francisco to New York in twelve days, rather than the three months it took during the winter by clippership making the passage around South America.

1859

The Mountain Messenger, a newspaper in Downieville, California, wrote, "Norwegian snowshoes have come into general use. By means of these Norwegian snowskates, a person can travel from point to point with as much safety, if not with the same speed and comfort, as he could in the summertime."

1861

The first ski races were held in California's Sierra Nevada, probably in 1861. According to *The Mountain Messenger*, the races were straight downhill and "speeds of 72 miles an hour were reached." The races were straight downhill because of the tremendous length of the skis—up to twelve feet—and because only toe straps were used. (Norheim's heel binding, while it was being used in Norway, for some reason did not find its way to the United States until late in the 19th century.) At the same time, ski-jumping contests were held. A Norwegian named Andrew Jackson was reported by *The Mountain Messenger* in 1863 to have jumped 150 feet.[2]

1863

The gold miners in America were the first men in history to use ski wax. Each man had his own secret recipe, and ski wax was also sold in local general stores.

1867

The first American ski club—the Alturas Snowshoe Club—was formed in Laporte, California.

1870–1905

The interest in skiing really began to spread. Norwegians were skiing in Colorado, Wisconsin, Minnesota, Montana, and the Dakotas. In 1882, the first ski club in the east was formed—Skiklubben. It was

---

[2] It is impossible that anyone on twelve-foot skis, fastened only with toe-straps, could have accomplished a jump of 150 feet, as The Mountain Messenger claims. Later, in the 1880's, it was claimed that speeds of 72 miles an hour were reached, but this also is highly exaggerated.

The complete skier, 1907.
Note hooded cape,
single pole. She carries
a knapsack on this
cross-country journey.

founded by Norwegian settlers in Berlin, New Hampshire. In 1901, they changed the name to Nansen Ski Club. More ski clubs were founded in the midwest, mainly around Minneapolis, Minnesota, and Ishpeming, Michigan. In Redwing, Minnesota, Mikkel Hemmestveit, another Morgedal boy, set a world jumping record in 1891 with a 102-foot-leap. His brother Torjus beat the record by one foot at Redwing in 1893. Both men had been taught to ski by Sondre Norheim.

In the winter of 1891, the Norwegians established the first ski association in the United States—the Ski Association for the Northwest—with headquarters in St. Paul, Minnesota. In 1904, the American Ski Association was founded, again by Norwegians, this time with headquarters in Ishpeming. The first president was Carl Tellefsen of Trondheim. Aksel Holter of Oslo was appointed secretary. In 1905, Holter published the first *American Ski Yearbook.* It covered the year's ski competitions—mostly jumping events with a handful of cross-country races. Virtually all the competitors were Norwegians.

And so it went, a sprinkling of Norwegian disciples of the snows spreading the gospel everywhere they went. Nansen's account of his historic trip on skis across Greenland was excitedly read by mountaineers in Germany, Austria, and England. An Austrian named Zdarsky experimented with a way to turn one's skis on steep slopes and came

*Three jumpers atop
Holmenkollen jump in
1906. Equipment
is the latest word,
including reed bindings.*

up with the stem turn and its old-fashioned variations.

In Norway, using the Norheim heel binding, racers from Morgedal added finesse to the sport by making elegant turns around trees and bushes. This they called *slalaam* from *sla*, which means a "smooth and slanting hill," and *laam* or track—a track down a smooth hill.

The remainder of skiing history is commonly known. Sir Arnold Lunn, the noted English devotee of the sport, introduced *slalaam*, which he had been watching for years in Norway, to alpine Europe. In 1923 he substituted poles for trees in a race in Switzerland, and the idea of slalom racing took hold, eventually evolving into the complicated sport that it is today. In fact, it has probably become too complicated and Lunn, now in his eighties, is spearheading a movement to take slalom back to what it was at its beginning, an uncomplicated race on uneven terrain around natural obstacles.

In the twenties, Norway still reigned over the world of skiing. At the first Winter Olympics, held in Chamonix in 1924, Norway took all of the gold medals and all of the silver and bronze medals except one, which went to Finland. The ski events were jumping and cross-country; it was not until 1930 that slalom and downhill were included as competitive events by the International Federation de Ski, and not until 1936 that they were included in the Winter Olympic Games held that year in Garmisch-Partenkirchen. In 1950, giant slalom was added

*Axel Henriksen turns
a complete somer-
sault on skis during
a meet at Duluth,
Minn., 1913.*

to the Olympic skiing roster.

Thus Norway, a nation on skis, gave birth to the sport as we know it today. In my youth, and in the lives of my parents and grandparents and their forebears, skis were as much a part of daily existence as was food.

Outside of the cities, skis were the only means of locomotion when the snows lay deep. Doctors used them to visit their patients. Vicars used them to get to church on Sunday and to make their daily rounds. When the snows were too heavy to rely on horses, everyone skied to church.

After services, the congregation would gather on the church hill. There would be races and tricks on skis; events that served to brighten the dim weeks of winter in the remote villages.

Skis were used for logging and for hunting, and for any work that took men into the deep woods. Boys and girls and their teachers skied to school for at least three months out of every year.

A Norwegian writer has put it very aptly:
There are three lines running through Norwegian history;
one is the furrow scored by the peasant's plowshare.
The second, the wakes of the Norwegian ships across
the seven seas.
The third, the ski tracks that girdle the Earth.

Before the turn of the century, visitors who came to Norway wrote home about the Norsemen who flew through the air like "birds with wooden wings," and how miraculous it was to watch them land softly on the snow after what was apparently an attempt at suicide. Wrote one correspondent, "In Norway, the kids are born with skis on."

Stein with slalom skis he used in 1952 Olympics. Center, Jakob Vaage with world's longest skis (12'3"). Right,Birger Ruud with jumping skis he used in 1936 Olympics.

APPRENTICE YEARS

I WAS NOT BORN WITH SKIS ON, of course, but I might as well have
been. My family was completely involved in skiing and had been
from the turn of the century. Skiing was meant to be my life. There
was never any doubt about it. I think I decided this when I was very
young. I loved the life my parents lived in our home near Oslo's skiing shrine, the Holmenkollen. It was a house that was constantly
filled with their skiing friends. There was always laughter and warmth.

My father, a great practical joker, had the gift of gathering people
around him. He was not a big man, but he walked with snap, straight-
backed, the picture of a man who took care of himself physically. He
was a kind of hero in Norway, an athlete of prominence who had become a successful businessman in the world of modern skiing. In this
atmosphere I grew up, knowing that one day his world would probably be mine. It was almost too perfect; there was very little conflict
in my childhood, except in deciding where I wanted to go in athletics.

I remember, at the age of seven, being aware of my father's glorious
trophies on the mantel above the fireplace and wondering what sort
of athlete I would become. In the middle of the top row stood a beautiful silver statuette of the perfectly built body of a gymnast. Would I
become a gymnast like him? Or a cross-country skier? He had many
trophies garnered in cross-country competition. Or a jumper? He had
won the treasured Ladies' Cup in the Holmenkollen. It was too much
to think about. I could make my choice another time. In the mean-
time, I would take a sauna bath in the room downstairs that my father
had built because he believed that you could never become a great
skier unless you took a sauna bath two or three times a week.

My father, Marius Eriksen, had not been born to skiing, although
he had been raised in Skien, in Telemark, which is the very heart of
the birthplace of the sport. His father, a successful metalsmith who
made finely designed ornamental iron and copper work to order,
moved his family from Arendal on the Skagerrak coast to Skien when
my father was quite young. He quickly became absorbed in learning
how to ski because it was the predominant sport in Telemark, and
all of his friends were very adept at it.

At the same time he became an outstanding gymnast—a member of

Marius Eriksen, Sr.,
in the back yard
of the family
home near Holmenkollen.
Stein's father was
in his thirties when
this snapshot was taken.

the Norwegian Gymnastic Team that competed in the Olympics in Stockholm in 1912.

However, skiing was his first love. In his late teens, Skien became too confined for him; the limited life of a small town was not what he wanted. Like other young men before him, he went to the big city Oslo, where he felt there were greater opportunities to pursue his sports career, get the best coaching, and at the same time find a way of life more suited to his temperament.

With his record as one of Norway's great athletes, he was able to find a job with Gunerius Petersen, at that time one of Oslo's largest department stores, as the manager of its new sports department. He took on the job with enthusiasm, building up its selection of ski equipment, and at the same time he kept up with his racing so that his name was constantly before the Norwegian public.

My mother and father met in the early twenties. Raised in a suburb of Oslo, she loved to tour—to ski on those cross-country trips that are the favorite pastime of most Oslo residents. In fact, it was on one of those tours that she met my father. They were married and she was swept into his skiing life, so much so that she organized and became the first president of the Ladies' Slalom Club of Oslo.

In 1924, Father began experimenting with a device that could be mounted on the skis to hold one's boots. For almost a century skis had been mortised. That is, a slit was put through them from edge to edge so that a strap or piece of metal could be slipped through that held the toes of the boots. In the twenties, this was the binding that everyone in Norway used, a piece of iron that went through the ski and was bent up on each side.

Marius Eriksen changed all of this by inventing a mountable toe-piece, the first of a number of changes he made that helped revolutionize skiing equipment. He was a constant tinkerer. In fact, one of the memories of my childhood, something I still dream about, was his workshop in the basement of our home where he was constantly making some gadget or other. Here was where he worked on our skis, taught us all about mounting bindings, how to repair skis, and how to wax. Filing edges was an art that I learned from him. Under his watchful eye, I mounted my first pair of bindings at the age of nine, and have done it myself ever since.

Father's patented toe irons screwed into the tops of the skis, allowed the skis to retain full strength, and could be moved to suit the wearer. It was a simple invention, but it became a boon to the skiers of the twenties and thirties. With the money earned from selling the patent, Father built the house that my brother and I were brought up in. After I was born, and against the advice of all of his friends, he gave up his secure job with Gunerius Petersen to open his own sport shop

Stein's mother during a skiing trip in Austria. Photo taken in the Twenties.

at Akersgaten 16, in Oslo. The shop, now at Akersgaten 21, together with another shop, is run by my older brother, Marius, Jr.

In my childhood, Akersgaten 16 was a second home to me. I learned an enormous amount about skiing just from watching how the store was operated. Here was where the leading sports figures of Norway gathered—the cross-country men and the jumpers and the few down-hill skiers. Just being around these god-like men was like an idyl for me.

Father was a devotee of alpine skiing and had, in fact, visited the shrine—St. Anton am Arlberg—many times, where he became a close friend of the acknowledged *meister*, Hannes Schneider. One day he returned home from Austria with what must have been one of the first pairs of steel-edged skis. Immediately he disappeared into his workshop, made a few changes, and with encouragement from my mother, decided he would go into the ski manufacturing business.

Marius Eriksen's "Streamlines," fully laminated, with steel edges, became the best-known and most sought-after skis in Europe during the thirties and forties. Everyone used them, recreational skiers and racers alike. They were not as popular in Scandinavia where downhill skiing was relatively new, as they were in the alpine countries of central Europe. Much of their success in that part of the world must be attributed to Willy Bogner, Sr., who is best known today, perhaps, as the man who glorified the female form by using stretch fabric in ski pants.

In the thirties, Bogner was Germany's most famous jumper and cross-country racer. He was also a slalom expert of some repute. My father and he were introduced by Willy's trainer, who had competed against my father in the early days. Despite the difference in their ages (my father was twenty years older) they took an instant liking to each other and Willy was virtually adopted as a member of the family. Father hired him as representative for Eriksen Skis in Central Europe.

I remember those years with great fondness. Mother was a beautiful, cheerful woman. But she was tough-minded. She ran our house and at the same time, served as my father's good right hand in the ski business. In fact, when Father became ill in 1940, she ran the shop and supervised the ski manufacturing with very little help. During the Second World War, with my father's increasing illness, the entire burden of the business fell on her shoulders. When Marius and I were growing up, she was insistent that we keep up with our school-work despite our intense desire to do nothing but ski and follow Willy Bogner around.

Willy spent part of every winter with us during the thirties. He trained in Norway and competed every year in the Holmenkollen. He was a good jumper, but he had one discouraging fault—at least to Marius and myself who were connoisseurs, as are most Norwegian boys, of the fine art of jumping. While his leaps were always good, he usually landed dragging one hand, which of course cost him penalty points. Yet in Norway he was one of the few central Europeans to be considered equal to the top Norwegian skiers in jumping and cross-country.

He was an excellent downhill and slalom skier. One of my earliest memories is of Bogner coming to Norway to demonstrate slalom and the small disaster that followed. My father met him in Oslo, and with a couple of pairs of Eriksen skis gracing the rear of Father's sports car, the two of them drove to our house before heading to the Galdhöppig-gen hill where Willy was to demonstrate. But father, who had placed the skis straight up in the rack, forgot that they were there. As he drove into the garage, there was a resounding crash. The skis had been neatly clipped in two by an overhang. The skis were prototypes; there was no time to fix them or replace them. So Bogner borrowed a pair of cross-country skis with thin profiles and no steel edges and demonstrated slalom turns with as much finesse as if he had been on regular steel-edged skis.

Outside of my family and a few people in Norway, the story of the

Stein's mother and father on a ski holiday at St. Anton am Arlberg in the early 1930's.

friendship between my father and Willy Bogner is not well known. To my parents, Willy was like an elder son. When we were very small, we were delighted to be carried around on his shoulders every evening before we went to bed—and to watch him very carefully as he made his preparations before training or competing. My father and he were very close, but as the war years drew nearer they began to drift apart. In 1941, after the invasion of Norway, Bogner, a German soldier, found himself a member of the enemy occupying force stationed in the country that had nurtured his skiing growth. He contacted my father. Although it hurt them both terribly, they told each other, "Now we must go our separate ways; we have our own duties to our countries."

It is said that Bogner developed a reputation for being "a good Norwegian" while he was with the occupation forces, by getting his skiing friends out of prison. Later, he was sent to Russia.

In 1946, my brother, despite having suffered severely at the hands of the Germans, decided a *rapprochement* was necessary. He flew to Munich for a reunion with Bogner.

Jumping was his first love. Stein, age seven, at Nystuen in Norway.

In 1950, my father and Willy Bogner met for the first time in twelve years. Despite Bogner's pre-war popularity, anti-German feeling in Norway was still high, so we arranged a reunion in Copenhagen. I remember that it was July and that we sat on the beach of a hotel near the Danish capital and had lunch together. It was the last time Willy and Father saw each other; father already was severely ill and died the following September.

I have often wondered about the friendship between the two. I think that what may have brought them together was the similarity of their backgrounds and the delightful sense of humor each had. Bogner's father, who like my paternal grandfather, had been a metalsmith, lived in the small town of Traunstein, in Bavaria. Willy, as a youth, had cut his ties with Traunstein and escaped to Munich, where like my father who had escaped to Oslo, he thought opportunities would be greater for him. I like to think that some of Willy's inspiration to continue with skiing came from Father, who had a dynamic effect on all his friends.

He certainly had it on his sons. As we lived in the hills outside of Oslo, Father made sure that we had a little ski jump and slalom hill in our own back yard. I may have been three or four years old when I first got on skis. Later, I remember, Marius and I practiced in the evenings, using Mother's candles to light up the little jump. On windy nights, the candles would usually blow out before we hit the take-off so that we would land in the dark, which we considered very exciting. Instead of an inclined out-run, Father built the jump so that we landed on the flat. When we argued with him that jumps were not built like that, Father said, "Your legs will get stronger," and that was the end of the argument.

Despite the family ski business, we were not pampered with new equipment. Marius and I were taught to appreciate what we had, and so we looked forward with eagerness to Christmas when we might be fortunate enough to get new skis. I remember Christmas Day of 1937 very well, because that was the day I was given new skis and promptly went out and broke them.

Snow had covered the ground in the first fall of the season, and Father had built the ski jump. With my shiny new skis, I climbed the inrun, ready to take my first jump. I took off into the air, thinking that it was a good leap, stood up, and felt secure. Then down I came. Just before making a stop turn I was thrown forward into the snow. Lying there, I couldn't understand what had happened until I uncovered my skis and discovered I had hit our flagpole, which had been taken down to be painted. And there were my precious new skis with both tips broken off. I couldn't have been more unhappy; I cried, I think, all day, until Father agreed that the accident was unforeseen and that I would get an identical new pair of skis.

I learned to ski without cable bindings. Until I was twelve, I used a combination cross-country and jumping binding, which was another

idea of Father's. It helped me improve my balance and judgement so that when I finally was given a pair of cable bindings, control became very precise.

Between the ages of five and nine, jumping was my favorite sport. I won my first prize at seven—a silver cup that stood four inches tall. It was given to me because I was the youngest competitor and both of my jumps were a respectable forty-five feet. Compared to the cups racked up by Father and by Marius, who was beginning to do very well in junior competition, mine looked puny indeed. But to me, it seemed bigger and better than theirs—especially when I closed my eyes and dreamed about it.

Another memory of my childhood: my first leap off a "big" jump. Near our house was the Midstubakken ski jump, next to the Holmenkollen. It was a 200-foot jump and at the age of nine I had first climbed the hundred steps of the inrun with my skis on my shoulder just like the champion jumpers did. But when I reached the first level, lacking courage, I turned around and walked down again. I'm sure that I did this at least a thousand times, until one cold winter night when I went to the jump with Marius, who was then a confident teenager and had several times leapt more than 120 feet. I was then eleven, and on this night Marius was going to practice, and in my heart I knew that he would jump, but that I would walk down again.

The hill was lit, and I followed Marius slowly up to the first level. Then Marius commanded, "Put your skis on."

Unwilling to appear cowardly before him, I did. Then everything happened quickly, before I had a chance to reconsider. The tips of my skis were in the track leading to the lip of the jump; a slight shove by Marius and I was on my way. I passed the point of no return. Was I dreaming? No, this time it was real. There came the edge of the take-off, and I was in the air. Automatically, I assumed the proper form. But fearful, I was a little late in my timing, and I suddenly hit the snow—the shortest jump ever accomplished on the Midstubakken. I rolled over and over in the snow, laughing all the while, and even before I came to a stop in the transition of the outrun, I had planned my second jump. My fear had disappeared. There stood Marius grinning at me with the faith in my ability that I had lacked.

This question of faith in ourselves and the ability to win or lose with grace was something that our parents tried to instill in us when we were young. I was seven when I first entered a slalom race. I had a good first run, but during the second run, I crossed my skis just before the finish line and fell. I remember crying, not because I was hurt, but because of my disappointment. Father put his arms around me and said, "It is better to win once in a while than all the time."

These values sound old-fashioned today, but he truly believed that one competed for the enjoyment of it and that being a good sport was more important than winning.

I never cried again over a lost race—at least, not so it could be seen. I have often been hurt inside. Or annoyed at myself for making mistakes. But hardest to learn was to embrace or congratulate the winner, knowing deep inside that *IF* I hadn't taken a gate too low, I would have been in his place. To lose with grace is what my father taught me.

Every week, my mother gave me enough money to buy a train ticket to take me to school outside Oslo. If I were tempted to buy candy or ice cream with it, then I had to walk or ski to school. In the winter, I was well supplied with candy for I skied to school almost every day. In the evenings I would take a downhill run to Oslo to attend gymnastic classes.

From the age of eleven on, gymnastics had become routine. My mother and father, had decided that I needed more muscle on my body; I was a skinny child. For several years before the war, Odd Bye-Nilsen, a champion gymnast, had established classes in Oslo for youngsters who were interested in this kind of instruction. When the war came, he rented a home in the capital where the classes were continued in secret. We met each night for an exercise session, then practiced acrobatics, using the parallel bars and horses and other gymnasium equipment. For a while, Bye-Nilsen sponsored an elite children's team that gave exhibitions throughout Norway. I was a member of this team. After Norway's invasion, the team was disbanded, but the classes continued.

I was in my early teens when the war came to Norway with its violence and the fierce non-compliance of my countrymen with German

occupation forces. Early in 1940 my brother disappeared, leaving intimations at home that he was going to try to get to Great Britain. After two attempts, in which their fishing boat was turned back by bad weather, Marius and several of his skiing friends made their escape from Aalesund, a village on the Atlantic Ocean.

Had they turned back a third time, they would have been captured, for the Germans had been tipped off that Aalesund was being used as an escape route. Other tough Norwegians had tried to join the Allied forces by using fishing trawlers, some commandeered at gun-point. Not all the escapes had been successful; the passage to the British Isles was a rough one, constantly patrolled by German aircraft. Thus our close neighbor and friend Thorleif Arentz lost his life. But Marius and his friends made it, and he was one of the first to join the newly-formed Norwegian Squadron of the Royal Air Force.

The wartime saga of my brother Marius is well-known in Norway, where he is a national hero because of the fight he carried on against the Germans and because of his skiing accomplishments. Almost a year had passed before we knew that he was safe in Great Britain, and not until the war had ended that we knew the full story of his odyssey. From Britain, he was sent to Canada for flight training during the winter of 1940–41. Stationed near Toronto, he spent his leave time skiing. If you check the records of the 1941 ski-jumping contests at Dartmouth, you'll find his name listed as a competitor. Qualified as a Spitfire pilot, he spent two years in the skies over Great Britain and the continent, where he shot down twelve German planes. In 1943, instead of taking a well-earned leave, he substituted for a comrade who was getting married. A stray bullet from a Focke-Wulf fighter hit his plane, which exploded in mid-air. The last thing Marius remembered was pulling the handle to release the hatch, and the handle coming off in his hand. By some miracle he was thrown clear, his clothes in flames. There was a hole in the top of his parachute. To this day, he has no idea how the parachute opened. He was only partially conscious as he came down over Holland.

Marius landed in a field with most of his clothes burned off. Some Dutch farm girls had watched him come down and as he landed they rushed to him with sheets. They covered him, and took him on their bicycle so that he could try to make his escape. But he was picked up by a German patrol.

The Germans were unable to believe that they had captured a Norwegian flier, having no knowledge, at least in Holland, that Norwegians were flying for the RAF. Marius was tortured by the Nazis for forty-eight hours during which they plunged his burned body into hot and cold baths. But he stuck to his story. Later he was removed to a hospital and then to a prison camp where he remained until the war

At eleven Stein shows the confidence that would help him during his racing years.

Norwegian champion gymnast Odd Bye-Nilsen instructs a physical conditioning class for alpine racers after the war. Stein is second from right.

ended.

The family heard through clandestine sources, first that he was missing in action over Holland, and then later that he was in a German *lager*. This was confirmed by the International Red Cross, so that at least we knew that Marius was safe. Later, through the Red Cross, we received occasional letters from him. With the war's end, he was released. He had left Norway five years earlier as a sixteen-year-old, still—in my parent's eyes at least—a callow teenager. He returned as a twenty-one-year-old lieutenant in the Norwegian Air Force, very much a man. For a while he served in the Air Force as a flight instructor, then resigned from the service to join my father and mother in their ski business.

During those war years, I was having my own problems. Too young to fight, or to follow Marius, and still in school, I occupied my spare time with skiing. I had decided to become an alpine racer through a quirk of circumstance. Father, for one, had switched his interests to alpine skiing. And for myself, I was finding downhill racing more exciting than jumping. I was never able, it seemed, to win jumping contests, but I was taking first places in slalom.

It was when I was eleven or twelve, I think, that I hung up the jumping skis for good. I had entered a jumping competition between the schools in our area and had placed second on a pair of jumping skis that I had taken great pains to prepare with just the right kind of wax. Then, after it was over, I discovered that the winner had taken the event on a pair of battered cross-country skis. That did it for me.

After the invasion, all skiing competition ceased. The Germans had apparently decided that any skiing events held strictly between Nor-

An ardent gymnast, Stein demonstrates an exercise for balance and leg strengthening. Picture was taken just after Second World War.

wegians would foster the spirit of nationalism. So they forbade any contests unless they or the *Hird* (Norway's collaborationist Hitler Jugend) took part. Naturally, none of us would have anything to do with the *Hird*, who we considered unspeakable because they had deserted our king and country when what we needed most was to draw together against the Germans. But to keep ourselves in shape we organized illegal slalom races deep in the forest around Oslo.

We were nearly caught at it more than once. I distinctly remember a confrontation on one of our remote hills between six *Hird* members and twelve of us who had been practicing slalom. The odds were on our side, two to one, and they withdrew. Had there been a fight, I think we would have killed them because we hated them so much. We were very close in those days—a band of young patriots in an occupied nation.

I think the war implanted in those of us who were young skiers a sense of responsibility to Norway. Somehow we developed the drive to go before the world when international competition was again possible and bring our country back to the position it had held before the war.

When the war ended, I was seventeen, strong physically and tough mentally. I had an intense desire to make the kind of name for myself that my father and brother had made. In 1939 Marius had been the sole Norwegian alpine hope at the FIS games in Zakopane. He had been thwarted by the war. I felt that he and I should carry on together. In 1947 he became the Norwegian Slalom Champion, and in 1948 we both made the Norwegian Olympic team.

It was my parents' proudest moment. And the end of my apprentice years.

Among the first of Stein's big wins was the 1951 Lauberhorn at Wengen, Switzerland. On these pages— an album of pictures taken during that upcoming year. Above, Stein with Norwegian coach Kjell Borge Andersen, center, and George Schneider. Right, signing autographs at a post-race banquet.

40

After the Wengen
victory, a hoist in
the air by Karl Molitor,
left, former Swiss
racer and now a ski
boot manufacturer.
On the right is one
of the grand old men
of European skiing—
Ego Gertsch, founder
and president of the
Wengen Ski Club.

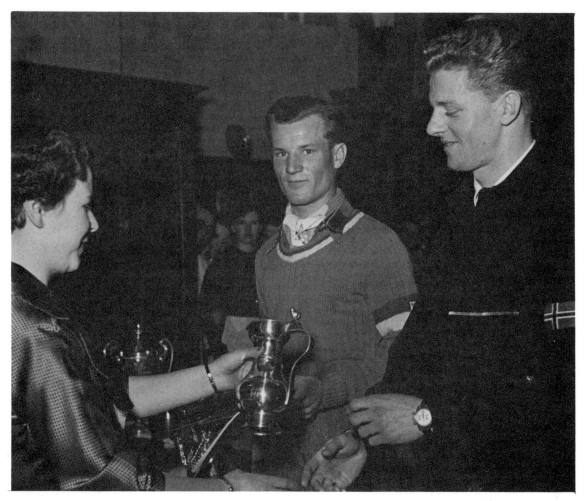

*More memorabilia.
Left, an affectionate
hug from Maria
Bogner after a win at
Badgastein.
Above, trophy
presentation at
Wengen.
On Stein's right is
Austria's Othmar
Schneider, now
a successful
ski school director
in the United States.*

RACING YEARS
Olympics, 1952

FEBRUARY 19, 1952. The steep, gullied hill called Ródkleiva, just outside Oslo. I am climbing it, side-stepping carefully past fifty gate combinations. I study the course and plan my race more carefully than anything I have ever done in my life. For years, it seems, I have been skiing Ródkleiva. Most of the time it has been at night, under lights, with fellow members of the Norwegian Olympic team. We have practiced, practiced, practiced until we know every possible variation in the terrain, every conceivable gate combination that we can set up. But always we have been alone.

But now we are no longer alone. Thirty-five thousand Norwegians are grouped like a gigantic horseshoe of humanity along the sides of the slalom *pistes* and around the runout. For today is the climactic ski event of the 1952 Winter Olympics and today slalom has returned to its native Norway.

My fellow Norwegians have waited a long time for this. After three decades, the winter Olympics have finally come home to the cradle of skiing. Six days earlier, the Olympic torch had been lit—not in Greece, but in Telemark, at the hearth of the house in Morgedal in which Norway's great skier, Sondre Norheim, had lived. At 10 A.M. on February 13, a historic torch-relay run had begun in Morgedal's town square. For two and a half days, ninety-four of Norway's best cross-country skiers had passed the torch from hand to hand over the 220 kilometers between Morgedal and Oslo. Finally, Eigil Nansen, grandson of the famed explorer, had run the last 400 meters into Oslo's Bislet Stadium, where to the constantly cheering crowd of 32,000 of his countrymen, he lit the Olympic flame.

The ensuing days had seen some of Norway's finest hours. Norwegians had won the Nordic Combination and the 18 km. cross-country in Holmenkollen; 130,000 persons, almost half of the population of Oslo, had watched Arnfinn Bergmann and Torbjorn Falkanger take gold and silver medals in jumping. A Norwegian, Hjalmar Andersen, had swept three gold medals in speed-skating. And I had contributed to the Norwegian triumph by winning the giant slalom at Norefjell.

Gold medal in the balance. Stein recovers during the 1952 Olympic Giant Slalom.

I had been fortunate at Norefjell. Eighty-six racers from twenty-six nations had competed. Among them had been the world's best—the legendary Zeno Colo of Italy (now thirty-three years old and still racing), Austria's Tony Spiess, Othmar Schneider, Christian Pravda, and Hans Senger—an almost unbeatable combination. Amidst these heroes, I had been a lonely figure, somewhat untried, for in the 1948 Olympics I had been able to do no better than twenty-ninth in slalom.

But in countering the sixty-six-gate course, everything seemed to work for me. I skied better than I ever had, taking the gates very closely. My speed was constant, I made no mistakes, and when the times were posted I had beaten Pravda by almost two seconds and Spiess by more than three. But, because Norefjell is more than ninety miles from Oslo, only a comparative handful of spectators (about 8,000) had shown up to see the victory. In the downhill, which took place a day or two later, I had the best Norwegian clocking for a seventh. Colo took the gold medal, unbelievably more than two seconds ahead of Schneider and Pravda.

But while my teammates—Guttorm Berge, Per Rollum, Gunnar Hjeltnes—and I were at Norefjell, we worried about Ródkleiva. When we left Oslo, it had been fearsome—blue ice, stumps, rocks—a course that we viewed with skepticism. I returned to Oslo, thankful that I could sleep in my own bed in my mother's house and rest well before the slalom. The following day, one member of each team was selected to ski Ródkleiva and report its condition to his teammates. With elation, I told Berge, Rollum, and Hjeltnes, "It's great!" The hill had been transformed in a week's time by several hundred Norwegian Army troops from a horrible "skating rink"—to a perfectly prepared slalom hill.

So now I am on Ródkleiva and 35,000 Norwegians watch my every move. As I climb, many thoughts occur to me. First, it seems totally ironic that so many of my countrymen have turned out to watch an event that they once wanted banned from the winter Olympics as not being pure skiing. So today, perhaps, I will be the one to finally bring slalom back to Norway; I must carry on in the tradition of Sondre Nordheim and of my father and my brother. The thought makes me tense. I turn my mind to the job at hand—concentrating on the gates and how I will ski them.

There are approximately sixty gates in all. The combinations are very cleverly arranged along the course, which is about 1400 feet long with a vertical drop of some 540 feet. It seems to me that they are difficult, and I can almost hear the other racers near me saying to themselves: "If I take this gate from the right, it will be safe. But I can go into it from the left . . . it will shorten my track by a few feet . . . but I am taking a chance if I do it. If I fall I am out of the Olympics, probably forever."

As I climb I am in doubt, myself, about some of the combinations,

*Victor and victorious.
An embrace for Italian
racer Zeno Colo
who had just won
Olympic Downhill.*

47

but I know that in some subconscious way the doubts probably will be resolved by the time I am in the starting gate.

Then other doubts begin to crowd my mind. Although I feel good, and know that on a day like this—sunny, warm, the kind of day that inspires—I can win, I still feel like an outsider. Here again are others who are as good as I am and possibly better—Zeno Colo, the Olympic downhill champion, and the formidable Austrians, Schneider, Spiess, Senger, and Pravda. I think to myself, "Among them I am the dark horse. Imagine if I make it today, have the best time, and win. What will everyone say?"

Then I think about disaster. "What would they say if I fell. I just cannot fall. I have to stand up. Maybe I will be thrown back and outside of a gate . . . not fall . . . but lose valuable seconds. Then what? Then I will go wild during the remaining part of the course. My concentration will break. I will fall and fall again. Or maybe I will fall where the course is steep and slide past four or five gates."

Then I think, "How are the bindings? Are the longthongs strong enough, or are they worn? Will they break when I need them the most?" I reach over and check my bindings.

My thoughts are terrible. But they exist and I know they exist for every one of the eighty-seven racers who are skiing today. But the closer I get to the start, the more they begin to fade away. In the minutes before the start, it all changes, and I concentrate again on the course and my technique. Again I am where I was twice before this week, at Norefjell in the giant slalom and downhill races—alone.

Earlier, as I was climbing, the 35,000 spectators meant much to me. I race for them, I thought. I have to give what they ask for—utmost effort. Falling is out of the question. Now, even the spectators fade away; they are like so many wooden poles in the snow and I am alone before the start.

The loudspeaker: "Five minutes until the start of the men's slalom."

I lie down on my back in the snow feeling the heat of the sun on my face. The sky is very blue. I shake my legs. My muscles are loose and ready. The same thing is happening today as on the other days of competition at Norefjell, but everything seems so much more concentrated. From where I lie close to the starting gate, I can see half the course. Before the giant slalom and downhill I could see only the first two gates from the start. Here I am in the middle of it all—starters, press, loudspeakers, doctors, trainers, coaches, spectators, friends, everyone is here and yet they are a blur, only a kind of backdrop in my mind.

I get up, throw the skis on my shoulder and walk slowly up to the ladder that leads to the ramp that has been built to provide the requisite height for the start. I climb the ladder.

The starter: "Numbers 1, 2, 3, 4, 5, 6, and 7 get ready."

I am nervous again. Despite the warmth I suddenly feel cold. The last meet is coming to an end—my last Olympics. Now I must give

Consultation on Rødkleiva, above. Stein talks with Colo, center, and Switzerland's George Schneider, before the slalom start. Left, a happy trio after the giant slalom. Stein is flanked by silver medallist Christian Pravda, left, and bronze medal winner Tony Spiess, right.

God jul, og et godt Olympiaår. Hilsen Ste...

all that I have. Do I have anything left to give? Did I drain myself in the past two races? I tell myself, "Shake it off."

I am on the starting ramp. With a wish for luck, I pat my friends on their backs. There is not enough space for seven men up here. I find a place on one end of the line, but there is hardly room for my skis.

Now the last thorough preparations. Place the boots carefully in the toe and heel irons. I am using a binding that I have designed myself for slalom skiing. I have confidence in it even though it will not protect me by releasing in a fall. I tighten the longthongs around my boots. They feel snug. Now the pole handle straps; they are strong.

Everything is in order. Except for my skis. There is some snow on my left ski and it has to be brushed off. This has no practical importance, but seeing the snow there bothers me. Both skis must look the same. I have to see the beautiful grain of the wood shining through the varnish equally on both skis. It's silly, I know, but suddenly very important.

The start is on the edge of the ramp so that the racers' feet are placed on the balance point. The lower legs press against a steel wand that bends to one side when the racer pushes off and starts the electric timers. As I watch a forerunner preparing, I realize that if I jump the gun before the word "go," it will have no effect on my time. The clocks start when I do. So I relax a little.

The forerunners are off and gone. Number one is in the starting gate. I am number three today, and before I know it, I get the one-minute warning. I am in the gate now—looking straight ahead, my mind concentrating on remembering every detail of the course.

"Fifteen seconds."

The sun reflects in a snow crystal on my ski tip. It almost blinds me —everything has been refined to its utmost clarity. I am ready for the explosion, knees touching the wand, a firm grip around my ski poles, my arms shake slightly. One ski is back against a board of the ramp for pushoff power.

I hear the starter breathing. Suddenly the grip on my shoulder becomes more firm. The measured count begins.

"Five . . . four . . . three . . . two . . . one . . . Go!"

Forward now. Relax. Take it easy in the first few gates. Now they rush past me, one after the other. I do not wait to make my turns as I do in giant slalom and downhill. I throw myself forward toward the next gate before I am completely through the one I am in.

I am eager today. Forward, there, over there. Now—high, up here. I am conscious of using all of my muscles. I must react quickly, quickly. I am thinking three gates ahead and planning my race. I cannot rest one-tenth of a second.

Post-olympic presents, above, were designed by an eleven-year old neighbor of the Eriksen family.

Cover, left, of a Norwegian men's magazine shows Stein in action before 1952.

. 2.   20 øre   AFTENPOSTENS OLYMPIAUTGAVE   15. februar 195

Steinvant

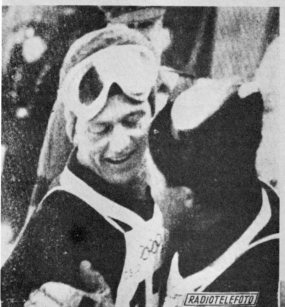

For OLYMPIAPOSTEN av Per Bjørn AMUNDSEN

Norefjell, 15. februar.

Stein Eriksen klarte i dag det som så mang
hadde håpet, men som så mange hadde fryktet ha
ikke skulle greie — med favorittens svære nerve
press over seg— han vant gullmedaljen til Norge
vår første olympiske gullmedalje i de alpine grene
Den 24-årige Ready-gutten slo nestemann, øster
rikeren Christian Pravda med 1.9 sekund, og det e
såvidt meget at man må kunne snakke om over
legen seier. Det var vill jubel ved TK-huset da Stei
skar over mål i voldsom fart. Like etter lød høyt
taleren: dagens hittil beste tid! Det er kanskje p
sin plass allerede nu å minne om at det er to timer
protesttid, men ennu har ingen snakket om noe so
helst galt oppe i løypa, så vi tør regne med gull
medalje til Stein Eriksen. De mest kjente løpern
er nu kommet inn, og man regner med at ingen a
de senere startende kan true nordmannen.

Fortsatt side 15

Olympia-ilden er
tent på Bislett

en olympiske ild tendes på Bislet av Frithjof Nansens sønnesønn.   Fot.: Susi Asa

*From the
OlympiÅposten,
February 15, 1952,
"Stein Wins."*

KOMMENTARER PÅ FEM SPROG

The first gates were placed in a line and easy to ski through. But I must not forget to concentrate. It is easy to lose the race in them—a pole between the legs and you are out of the Olympics forever. On these early gates, I lift one ski at a time and put it down on the snow angled in the direction of the next gate. Less turning this way, more speed.

Now Ródkleiva gets steeper. The gates are no longer in the fall line. They force me to turn more and I must push down more in the turns. My edges are sharp; they carve nicely in the firm snow. I touch the inside pole in each gate with my shoulder. It feels comforting to be so close to them. I know that my line is the shortest possible. A good course; I like it. I am at the midway point.

I breathe harder, forcing the air in and out of my lungs. But I am not yet tired. I approach the steepest part of the course. Careful, I must be more forward. If I sit back here I am out. Now the turns are sharper than ever. I am using more strength and am getting tired. Back and forth now, a difficult traverse. Will I be able to make it? Yes, my turns are still smooth. I am doing all right. "Everyone gets tired here," I say to myself.

My breath is shorter, my legs weaker. Keep your style, I say to myself. Keep forward, forward, there are only six gates left. I hold on the best I can in this steep section. It must have a forty-degree pitch right here before the finish line. I go through the last gate and pole violently toward the finish.

After I stop, I hang over my ski poles for several seconds trying to get my wind back. It is painful. My legs are trembling. Then, suddenly, my legs and heart start to function more naturally and my strength comes back.

The newspapermen rush toward me. So far, best time in the first run, they tell me. I can't believe it; maybe there is another chance for a gold medal for Norway. But the race isn't over yet. Hans Senger comes in and ties with me. Other racers are close behind.

No, the race is not over yet. Senger and I have to maintain our position, and in fact, to win I must ski faster than him. And the others will be going all out to cut seconds off their time in the second run. Spiess and Pravda are out. They have fallen. Schneider is three-tenths of a second behind me. Guttorm Berge is in sixth place and Per Rollum also has done well.

"Ten minutes until the start of the second run."

We climb again to the start. Timers are ready. Starters are ready. We step nervously around but nothing happens. There is a delay. Keyed up, the racers are annoyed. What a time for a delay. To wait ten minutes is like waiting for hours. Someone has protested on a gate halfway down the course. The problem is solved and number one takes off. Number two is gone, and it is my turn again.

I feel better than I did in the first run. Should I give it everything I have? "Don't take chances," I tell myself. Safe, smooth, and fast. But

*From the
OlympiAposten,
February 19,1952.*

a small voice inside of me says, "Beat them." It tells me, "Beat them all."

In the first gate I feel it all again—terrific. The reward of all of the years of hard training and discipline is paying off. I have skied the first half of the course better than in the first run. I approach the steep section again, first taking with ease some gates on the ridge. Barely I see the stand in which the royal family sits. It is going very smoothly.

Then, as impossibly as thunder out of the blue sky, the skis suddenly slip away from me. Screams from the crowd. I am thrown back and off balance heading away from the next gate. Almost falling, I throw myself around in a panic. My body feels weak. Is this the nightmare that I have often dreamed? No, it is really happening. In a daze, I am back on the course again. I have just saved myself from falling, but I know I have lost time.

Now I am not flexible and confident anymore. I am like a different person on my skis. But I am going to make it and I fight for every tenth of a second until I pass through the finish line knowing that there will be a gold medal winner, but that it will not be me. I did not deserve it; the course defeated me.

But the newspapermen and photographers again rush to me. My time is excellent, and I have a total good enough for a silver medal. Othmar Schneider, the peerless Austrian, has had a flawless second run, and he takes the gold. I am grateful to have second place; I had given all that was in me.

And here come Guttorm Berge and Per Rollum. We embrace and hold each other like comrades. Guttorm has taken the bronze for third and Per has placed eighth, and we are like three small children who have been given everything in the world they have wished for.

The triumph for Norway was complete. It was a profound comeback for Norwegian winter sports. In the days following the Olympics, I suddenly found myself elevated into a world hero. I was presented to King Haakon and Crown Prince Olav. And naturally there was a tempest of offers of various sorts from everywhere.

Now, I had to make some important decisions for myself. I could retire as the Olympic Giant Slalom Champion. I could accept some of the more tempting offers to turn professional. In the end, after some deep soul searching, I decided that there would be no drastic change in my training or future program. I was twenty-five years old, still young, I thought, and ambitious about skiing. Since 1950, and my father's death, I had worked with Marius in the family business. So I decided to stay with amateur racing and enter the 1954 World Ski Championships (FIS), which would be held in Åre, Sweden.

Upon reflection, it seems to me that my decision was influenced by the Norwegian attitude toward sports champions. To my countrymen, skiing is truly a way of life; there is very little of the commercial approach to the sport found in some of the European alpine countries and in the United States. I had done something useful for Norwegian skiing—and this really was my reward. Also, there was now great *esprit* among the members of the Norwegian Olympic team. We felt that we had made Norway the best slalom nation in the world. There was pride for us in having accomplished this; we had done something for our country.

With everything, however, I still had something to learn about the sport of skiing. It is always a shock to one's ego to realize how little one really knows. My shock came when I went to the United States in 1953 on an amateur contract to meet people, ski with them, and teach.

It was a sunny, clear morning, during the Christmas holiday season at Sun Valley. Along with five experienced members of the Sun Valley Ski School, I took the lift up to the top of Baldy, where two feet of snow had fallen during the previous night.

After having been a racer all of my life, powder snow was something new to me. In Norway, whenever there had been a fall of new snow, we would ice it down with water to make better practice conditions. As I got off the lift, I glanced down at my skis—stiff racing models with longthongs and my stationary bindings. That was the last I saw of them that day.

Immediately we headed down the mountain the shortest way, under the chair lift (where everyone could observe us), down toward a narrow catwalk and over into . . . nowhere. It was not possible to see. It was strange—this powder; deep and heavy. I tried a few wiggles, to get my skis to turn. They continued—straight ahead. The speed steadily increased. I was leading, of course; my new friends were behind me making beautiful turns. I began to feel concerned, approaching another catwalk at forty to fifty miles an hour and unable to turn my skis. And my friends were still behind me, waiting to see the famous technique of the Olympic gold medal winner. Something had to be done.

I forced my weight forward and down I went, of course, down deep into the powder snow. But that didn't stop me. Not at that speed. I continued rolling over and over and over until somehow I stopped. Covered with snow, I pushed up my goggles and struggled to my feet, looking for the rest of the group. Through his laughter, one of them, a famous American ski instructor, said, "Are you *really* Stein Eriksen?"

Yes, I was really Stein Eriksen. But I didn't know how to ski deep powder. So I immediately set out to learn. More than that, I learned from this incident that there always is something new happening in skiing; some challenge perhaps, or new technique, or new people to meet. And it confirmed my desire to stay with the sport and see where it would lead me.

American interlude. Stein and Christian Pravda as Sun Valley instructors during the winter of 1953. During that season, Stein took Roch Cup and North Americans.

WORLD CHAMPIONSHIPS, 1954

In 1953 it led to more training, and in 1954 to the international racing circuit. I had hoped to make the tour right up to the FIS Games in Sweden, but at the Lauberhornrennen in Wengen, Switzerland, I took one of the worst falls of my career. During the downhill I lost control, bounced from mogul to mogul on one hip, rolled over, and finally came to a stop. It seemed as if every part of my body were bruised, but fortunately no bones were broken. I was under treatment for five days in the hospital in Schruns, Austria, where we were to race next. I wondered what I would do. Psychologically, I was in the dumps, and with the FIS Games coming in a month, I knew I had to get back on the racing circuit. Although I placed second in giant slalom in Kitzbühel's Hahnenkamm, I fell in the slalom, after which Willy Bogner, Sr., said, "Stein, you are not going to race for a while. You are going home."

He was right, of course. I had always trained in solitude, except for the pre-Olympic workouts when the whole team worked together. So I went home, and practiced on Ródkleiva and Tryvannskleiva until I was satisfied that my timing and speed had come back. Meanwhile Christian Pravda and Othmar Schneider and the others raced at Chamonix. I knew I was right when, a week before the World Championships, I swept the slalom and giant slalom in Opdal, Norway. All my toughest competition was present.

So, we all met again in Åre, Sweden, in February 1954—almost the same cast that had been in Oslo two years earlier. Only the terrain had changed. And something had changed in me, too. Staying off the racing circuit had sharpened me tremendously. I was physically fit and not afflicted with the mental staleness that comes from too much racing. And I was up: I had won the last race before the FIS.

Slalom was the first event. In the first run, everything clicked with perfection and I arrived about a second and a half ahead of Pravda and Tony Spiess. Before the second run, I was lacing my boots when my coach came over to me and said, "Well, Stein, here is some con-

Start of Giant Slalom at 1954 FIS Games. Stein wears sweater given him by Pravda.

Number one. Atop the winner's podium at Åre, Stein is cheered by the crowd after taking the Giant Slalom. Left is runner-up François Bonlieu, right, bronze medallist Anderl Molterer.

centrated sugar and we'll just—you know—see you at the bottom." That was all. Just, "See you at the bottom."

On the second course, there was a hairpin gate midway down which actually was a trap. It had tempting open gates in front, so that if you weren't careful, you would go into it fast and then you were lost because you'd have too much speed to make your turn into the new direction. There, Pravda and Spiess exploded completely—just ran off the course. I had another good run and beat them for the gold medal.

In the giant slalom I ran number one, which isn't the best position to be in, by any means. Despite the forerunners, you are essentially making your own line and "pushing snow" as the racers say. Following my own theory, I took it easy in the first few gates so that I could save strength, find my rhythm, and then let go. The tenths of seconds I might have lost by doing this I made up farther on. That day, the giant slalom was so easy for me that when I hit the finish line, I said, "This was a fast one."

But then came François Bonlieu, a tiny French newcomer who skied as if a wolf were chasing him. He finished two-tenths of a second behind me, and I thought that my time was not so startling. Then Pravda, the most serious contender, finished with a time that was far slower than mine, and I knew that I was the World Giant Slalom Champion.

Downhill has never been my best event. In the downhill at Åre, something happened that I have never been able to explain satisfactorily. I came too low in a gate and landed in the crowd. But I got back on the course and placed in the first ten.

So at Åre, the ultimate victory for me—two gold medals. And another one as winner of the *combine*. I had reached the peak, and there was no question about my decision. If I continued in amateur racing,

anything I did from now on would be anti-climactic. Now, I would turn to the ski business as my father and brother had before me. I felt certain I could handle this. Despite all the intense training in the years after the war, my mother had insisted that Marius and I finish our studies. We had both taken degrees in Business Administration.

I was ready for the professional side of skiing. After I made my decision, there was a touching occasion in Oslo. My brother arranged a "Stein Eriksen Evening" at one of the capital's most famous auditoriums in honor of my departure from the ranks of amateur skiing. At the end of a number of tributes, I spoke, knowing that many Norwegian sports fans had been turned away at the door. Here, assembled before me in the crowded arena, were all my friends—wartime skiing companions, fellow members of the Olympic and FIS teams, my coach, Kjell Borge Andersen, who had done so much to building the postwar alpine teams.

I explained to them—and to the Norwegian people—why I had turned professional. I said I felt that I had accomplished the job my country had required of me; I recounted some of my personal experiences in training and told of the determination it took to bring me to the heights of racing. "Now," I said, "I must move on to other things." After it was over, and it was not an evening without tears, I thought to myself how sad it must be for an athlete to reach the summit, and not stopping at the top as I had, to walk slowly down the other side.

I was twenty-seven, and it seemed to me that the world was now very wide. It would not be an empty world as it is for so many athletes who spend their youths concentrating on the narrow segment that is their sport—and then have nothing left when they retire. In the world of skiing, there was much left to do.

SKIING AS A PROFESSION

AFTER THE FIS GAMES, there were a number of offers. The one that I chose was at Boyne Mountain, Michigan, where the challenge was not in the hills, which are comparatively tame, but in running a ski school properly and learning how to teach people to ski. At Boyne I began developing the philosophy of teaching and ski-school management that I continue to this day in my school at Sugarbush Valley, Vermont.

After two years, another change. Heavenly Valley, in California, made an offer that included the sports shop concession. So I moved to this rather unique resort on the shores of Lake Tahoe. This was good for another two-year period during which I became interested in the ski-wear business, which later led to the founding of an import firm.

At the same time, I ran the ski school at Portillo, Chile, during the northern summers. It was here that I met Dick Durrance again (the famed pre-war Dartmouth skier, now a cinematographer), who suggested that I might like to visit Aspen on my way home and talk with Whip Jones, who was planning to build a new ski area.

A deer hunt was arranged in Aspen that fall at the top of Aspen Highlands. I shot the only deer of the day. On the walk down, Whip wondered if I were interested in running the ski school for his new area. For me, Aspen was like home, for it was where I had trained myself for the 1950 FIS Games. A lonely Norwegian then, I had been welcomed by the townspeople and taken into their homes.

Within a few hours, I arranged to buy Whip's home in town and to set up a sports shop at the Highlands. I signed a contract to run the ski school for an amount considerably higher than at Heavenly Valley. Now Aspen was my home.

Six years later, at the behest of Damon and Sara Gadd who had helped transform the once marginal Mad River Valley of Vermont into a flourishing area with their resort at Sugarbush, I signed on to head the Sugarbush Ski School.

Portillo, 1954.
With a vacationing
Chilian family.
Emile Allais, who ran
ski school then is
at extreme right.

The past decade has been a full one. Since 1954, I have skied almost everywhere in the world where there is snow. And everywhere that I have been, I have found people full of curiosity about skiing. The Japanese, for instance, have been swept by a skiing craze. Until you see it, it is impossible to understand how thousands of them can pack into the Tokyo train stations on Friday night and Saturday morning, travel for many hours, then disembark to ski on slopes that literally are covered with so many skiers that there is no room to maneuver. And yet they do it and are so vitally interested in alpine skiing that they have fielded their own men's and women's alpine teams and have sent demonstrators to the World Ski Instructors' Congress.

In New Zealand and Australia, where I went to make a film with John Jay, there are snowfields unparalleled in their beauty and dimension. There was new excitement for me in New Zealand—tracking over white landscapes that had never been touched until we arrived.

There has been all of this, and at the same time, I continued to learn more about the sport. I had been a ski-school director right from the start; there had never been an interim period for me in which I could learn how to teach. But at the start I decided that skiers were interested in finding out how to ski in the simplest way possible. For myself, I could only use my own experience as a guide, and instead of burdening them with theory, teach them what I had taught myself or absorbed from others through the years.

*With mountain
priest Father Cruz
of Portillo.*

Best in the world. Only Toni Sailer has surpassed Stein's Olympic and FIS records.

At the same time, I had to develop a philosophy for managing a ski school. Ski instructors, by and large, are interesting people. Most of them are independent types, caught up in skiing because of the free, outdoor life it provides. Management of a ski school is like the management of any business—except that with a ski school, you are engaged in transmitting to a host of people, many of them raw, fearful beginners, your love for the sport. The skier, of course, only sees the facade, which is the instructor he works with, or myself at the morning and afternoon meetings. But somehow, he knows, after a day during which he has accomplished something that he could not do in the morning, that he has been well taught.

The hallmark of the good instructor is the ability to gain the trust of the learner, because only with confidence in himself and his teacher does the beginner cast his fears aside. It may be interesting for the reader to know what I demand of my instructors so that they will instill confidence in our pupils.

I insist that my instructors be immaculate in their dress—hair trimmed, pants pressed, boots shined every morning, their uniform parkas and T-shirts always clean. Every detail is important. Boot laces: black with no unsightly knots. Longthongs and ski-pole straps: just the right length so that they do not flap.

I ask my instructors to demonstrate in plain view of the pupils and to emphasize, in simple terms, the important movements in each maneuver. My instructors are able to imitate the pupil's mistakes, not for ridicule, but because the pupil otherwise cannot see what he is doing wrong. Then, during each lesson, the instructors add the salt—a slight challenge, perhaps a short run for novices, or pre-jumping for intermediates—so that the pupils begin to feel at home on their skis.

I demand discipline of my instructors, not only on the slopes, but in their après-ski lives as well. And I suggest that they continue learning, because in this way they refine their own style. Before the beginning of each season, for instance, I hold a daily instruction clinic for my own staff, and for any outsiders who care to attend. Each day for a week, there is drill on fundamentals, then, to cap each session, free skiing in which we run the mountain just for the joy of it. Clinics are held frequently during the season to keep the instructors sharp.

At Sugarbush, we teach the American Technique, with some slight modifications. But what I really try to instill in those who come to ski with us, is the essence of what I have learned in my thirty-five years of skiing.

What I have learned is that skiing is beauty. There is nothing that can equal the pride of accomplishment that comes from doing it well —the ability to handle every terrain change, every snow condition, with style and grace. The challenge: to reach the absolute climax of what is possible for you.

This is what I have learned. And this is what I teach.

Now, come ski with me.

Enjoyment ...
comes with
the ability to
handle speed ...

COME SKI WITH ME
2

A number of years ago, *Ski* magazine printed a picture of me in an extreme reverse-shoulder position. Underneath the picture was the caption: "Nobody skis like Stein."

I think that the caption probably was correct, because the style that has become synonymous with the way I ski was developed through many years of being on snow, patient self-training, and the building of my body to the point where I felt that I was coordinated enough to race against the world's best.

But I try to give my style another quality: gracefulness. To me, gracefulness on skis should be the end-all of the sport—what you, as a learning skier, should strive for. To come down a mountain, toes curled, teeth clenched, as you make each turn, is to deny to yourself the essence of skiing. Enjoyment, it is true, comes with the ability to handle speed. But how much more delight you will take in your skiing when you find your body working, almost eagerly, for you—your skis extensions of your own limbs, everything coordinated into one smooth whole.

It is true, of course, that the beginner is a long way from achieving such perfection. Let us face the fact that the beginner's main problem, usually coupled with a lack of physical strength, is fear, or to put it more exactly, anxiety.

Psychologists tell us that fear often works for us. Anxiety does not. Strangely enough, fear stimulates our adrenal system, and can get us ready to react in the well-known "flight or fight" phenomenon. Anxiety—an extreme form of apprehension—ties us up in knots and seems to have the adverse effect of limiting our coordination to the point where even the most simple maneuver can turn into disaster. Many skiers know the peculiar sensation that occurs when they get on skis for the first time each season. They gaze at the mountain, wondering if they remember how to turn, let alone control their speed. But the usual ritual helps—they slide into their skis, get on the chair-lift, ride to the top. And even as they wonder if they still retain the ability to slide down the ramp, they are doing it, coming to a stop, making their first turn of the season. Suddenly it all comes back, perhaps painfully at first, but by the time the day has ended, a sort of subconscious rote memory has taken over and they are beginning to coordinate again as well as they ever did.

INTRODUCTION

FEAR, THE STEIN TURN, AND WHAT I BELIEVE

The beginner, of course, has lots to be anxious about. The experience is initially frightening because he is working against all the physical laws. Reason tells him (wrongly) to cling to the hill; he puts his weight on an uphill ski, or sits back, and falls. The anxiety of challenging these physical laws overwhelms him; he is tense, completely unrelaxed, and so finds that his first experience on skis becomes a trial.

I am in absolute sympathy with the beginner. I have seen persons turn out for ski school completely petrified with fear and unable to make the most simple move; they are taking up the sport for social reasons, or because everyone else in their family is doing it. But they are so frightened they cannot enjoy themselves.

The challenge to me and my staff is to prove to them that skiing can be fun.

How, then, to overcome your anxieties about skiing? The answers are almost too simple. First, you must be guided, as a novice and even as an intermediate skier, by someone in whom you have complete confidence. You cannot do it by yourself. You must be willing to admit this and to put yourself into the hands of someone you trust. That "someone" should be a qualified professional ski instructor.

There is no *mystique* about what the ski instructor does. If he is good at his job, his main function is to dispel uncertainty. Uncertainty during the learning process —and it is as true in learning how to drive a car, for instance, as it is in learning how to ski—leads to those anxious moments when the body refuses to coordinate. The instructor provides a guided transition from step to step. And as you learn from him and accept his guidance, you become more at home on your skis, you extend your capability, you gain experience, and your anxiety shrinks away. It's as simple as that. And it works.

Secondly, in order to enjoy the sport you should be in good physical condition. I know that it is difficult for the average city dweller to accomplish this. But the alternative is the inability of your body to obey your mind's commands—no matter how sure you are that you can perform a certain maneuver. If the muscles refuse to cooperate, then fear again takes over. It is important that you come to the slopes relaxed and physically fit.

In fact, let's defer taking those first steps in skiing and discuss how I keep fit and how you can adapt my methods to your own way of life.

GET FIT WITH ME

W<small>HAT DOES SKIING REQUIRE?</small>

First, strong legs, which means strong thigh muscles, strong ankles, and flexible knees. Second, you must have good wind and a fair amount of coordination, balance, and concentration. If you build these, as a beginner you will enjoy your first days on skis more than you might think possible. And if you are a more advanced skier, your skiing will not be spoiled by fighting that feeling of tiredness and in-capability when you try to take that last run. Fitness is also an accident-preventive measure. Tiredness and loss of muscle control are a major source of accidents on the slopes.

But fitness is a year-around job. It isn't really enough to engage in what is referred to as "pre-season conditioning." A healthy outdoor life with some consistent form of exercise will do more for you than weeks of strenuous calisthenics before the season starts—exercises that you drop as soon as you get on skis.

Even the city person can rearrange his life a little. Give yourself a little additional time each day and walk more. Breathe the fresh air and use your legs. Try climbing stairs instead of taking elevators. Many women find modern-dance classes help their muscle tone, even though they know they will never achieve the grace of a Martha Graham. Run, if you can, perhaps in a nearby park.

If you live in the countryside, you are more fortunate. You can chop wood, you can bicycle, you can run. In Norway, running is a favorite form of recreation. In training, I ran twice a week: in the woods, through dry creek beds, down hills, over rocks, on logs, under bushes. Try to use the natural terrain variations. A half-hour a day on weekends is all that it takes.

The main thing is to be consistent. Try to exercise at least three days a week, if you can't find the time to do it every day.

Now, here are some exercises that I do for strengthening my muscles and for concentration, coordination, and balance.

FOR KNEES AND ANKLES

We know that these are fragile parts of the body. For skiing, ligaments and muscles must be especially strong and supple. Buy a jump rope and use it. First, jump on your toes to develop spring in your legs. Jump with both feet together, then one at a time. After you are able to accomplish this, lay out an area about two feet square and jump from corner to corner. This simulates turning on skis.

FOR KNEES AND THIGHS

1. Jump rope from a crouch (see illustrations). Use the rope to stretch the muscles of the legs by forcing against the rope and pulling with your arms. 2. With feet apart, raise up and sink down and hold it. There is an angle between legs and floor.

FOR THIGH MUSCLES

Back against the wall, thighs perpendicular and lower legs parallel to the wall. If your back is flat against the wall, not many seconds will pass before you realize the condition of your thigh muscles. Start by holding the position for five seconds. Then each day add two seconds. On this one, don't skip a day.

FOR THE STOMACH

This area can always stand a little reduction and trimming. As in the illustrations, lie on your back with arms stretched above your head. With one motion, lift the upper body and legs at the same time. Remain in this position a little longer than you think you can, then back to the floor. Increase the number of repetitions each day.

Another exercise for the stomach: On your back, arms to the side, legs straight, toes pointed. Lift the legs up to 90 degrees, let them down again so that they are about two inches above the floor, then up to 90 degrees again, and down. Repeat slowly as many times as you can the first day, then increase by one each day.

FOR PROPER BREATHING

An absolute must in conditioning, although we don't realize it. When starting down a challenging slope, we concentrate, look ahead, perhaps to a spot of difficult terrain—a sharp mogul or patch of ice. We inhale, get tense, and forget to exhale properly. The next challenge appears, and the next, and soon we are out of breath and forced to stop. If the body is not supplied with the proper amount of oxygen, the muscles tire, and the entire system becomes weakened. Proper breathing can be developed easily while we exercise. As you exercise breathe so that you can hear it. Inhale, exhale, inhale, exhale, and continue the exercise. This deep breathing alone will help your general body tone.

These are the basics. If you'd like to move on to something more difficult, try the exercises illustrated on these pages for concentration, coordination, and balance. You may find them difficult to begin with, but with a little practice you will enjoy your proficiency in them.
Feel fit? Muscles ready? If you've done all I've suggested, you'll come to the slopes feeling very special.

So let's begin.

FOR THE STOMACH
*Basic stomach-strengthening exercise
helps build stamina,
strengthens
carriage and posture.
Legs are lowered slowly to
within inches of the floor.
Start with six lifts,
increase by one each day.*

83

CONCENTRATION AND BALANCE
This one takes more strength and should be attempted after accomplishing less difficult exercises.
With feet together, jump a low bench as many times as you can. Then increase by one each day.

STRENGTH AND BALANCE
*This exercise
starts with a squat
jump, then legs
are stretched and
swung while the
body is held in posi-
tion with the
hands. Helps
strength and balance.*

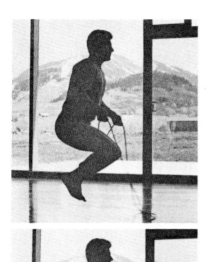

FOR KNEES, THIGHS
Use jump rope to aid conditioning. In this exercise jump on your toes, in a crouch. As you grow more proficient, alternate feet during each jump.

STRETCHING
Stretch leg muscles by using rope and forcing against it as shown in the illustrations.

ROPE EXERCISE
More complicated rope-jumping exercise involves jumping from corner to corner of an imaginary square.

COORDINATION
In this one, legs and arms work in opposition to each other. Aids coordination, strengthens stomach, legs, shoulders.

BEGINNING SKIING
A Word About Equipment

A<small>LMOST AS FRIGHTENING</small> as the initial step you take on the slopes is your first visit to a specialty ski shop. The array of boots, skis, and bindings laid out for you is bewildering. The price range, in skis for instance, goes from less than $30 to almost $200. What to select? How much to pay? What materials? Which of a dozen varieties of bindings to buy?

What has happened, of course, is that technology has invaded skiing. Where my father, in the thirties, made one ski, the "Streamline," there are now within each brand from three to more then a dozen models from which to choose. Metals, Fiberglas, and polyethylenes are used in ski manufacturing; the way materials are put together will have an effect on how the ski performs on the slopes.

Rather than enter into a technical analysis of ski equipment, here are a few general rules to aid you in your buying:

BOOTS

I consider a proper-fitting boot the skier's most valuable piece of equipment. The boot must operate as one with the foot—only then can proper control of the skis be achieved. Well-fitting boots aid the subtle edge control necessary for intermediate and advanced maneuvers. While there may be some room around the toes, the heel should fit snugly so that there is no lift inside the boot when you lean forward. The counter (the concave portion of the boot that fits around the instep) should be reasonably firm; this is the area that tends to break down first after the leather has been stretched by wet snow and the constant pressure of skiing. The more you pay for a boot, the better the quality of the leather will be and the more resistant it will be to stretching. Other tips: if you have problem feet—such as fallen arches—you might look for a boot with "canted" soles. These help keep the pressure off the inside edges of your skis by tilting the foot slightly toward the outsides of the skis. Consequently you will find that the problem of "catching" your inside edges—typical of flat-footed skiers—will occur less frequently.

Buckle boots or lace boots? Buckle boots have the added advantage of convenience, one can loosen them quickly after skiing, or even while riding a chair lift. Persons with problem feet may find them hard to fit as most models come as a single boot—no inner lace-up padded lining. (More expensive models have an inner boot.) Another tip: buy boot trees and keep your boots in them after skiing. They keep your boot soles rigid so that there will always be maximum contact with the skis.

SKIS

Here the price range is extreme. In general, the beginning skier should look for a ski that will work the best considering the buyer's weight and height. While the tendency these days is toward slightly shorter skis, the rule of thumb that a ski should be about a foot longer than a person's height still applies when the skier is heavy. For instance, a man who weighs 175 pounds and is six feet tall would do well to buy a ski that is at least six feet nine inches long.

Higher-priced skis have hidden and/or one-piece edges so that it is virtually impossible for the edges to pull out. Their bottoms may be of polyethylene, which is marketed under several trade names; the polyethylene helps the skis run better and they need less waxing. However, all skis need waxing, despite legend to the contrary. Wax helps preserve the bottoms and at certain temperatures helps the skis to slide.

Metal skis or wood skis or Fiberglas skis? Your choice here is a function of your pocketbook. Metal skis start at a price close to $100. They are generally more durable, and some models are easier to turn.

If you spend $100 or more for a pair of skis, you have made an investment. Make sure that the investment pays off: in other words, the manufacturer must stay behind the product and give you the service you deserve.

POLES

For length, the rule-of-thumb still applies: handles reach the arm-pit when the points rest on a flat surface. Poles should be light, the baskets firmly attached, the grip and strap comfortable *when you wear gloves*. Again, the choice is a function of price—and your skiing ability. A pole that is too short encourages too much forward lean of the upper body; too much bending at the waist. We try to avoid this in teaching skiing.

BINDINGS

Release bindings are the rule. It is impossible here to differentiate between the many types of bindings available on the market. For the beginner and intermediate skier, bindings must release forward and laterally. Always keep them in perfect working condition—free of rust or of the corrosive salt that may gather on them after a long car ride over heavily salted highways.

When buying equipment, another word of advice. As the ski instructor guides you on the slopes, so should a qualified salesman guide you through his ski shop. He will be interested in your budget, and most important, in your ability and level of skiing. Some skis, because of certain characteristics built into them, are for better skiers only. The wise ski-shop salesman knows this and will counsel you accordingly.

First Steps

Now THE MOUNTAIN LOOMS BEFORE YOU. As you get into your new bindings you glance up to watch skiers swivelling their way through the snow. They come to a grand, smooth stop, then skate off to a chair lift or T-bar for another run. Apparently everyone can handle any challenge; they are flushed, happy in their excitement over the snow that has fallen during the previous night. You wonder if it is at all possible ever to be like them—to make such glorious turns in the snow that is tinged this morning with sunlight. "Well," you say to yourself, "all I have to do is start," as the ski school bell begins to ring.

At first you will be concerned, not with that enormous mountain—but with a small portion of it. Here you will take your first steps and your first run, going ever higher and higher, until your instructor leads you to that grand, never-to-be-forgotten day when you will run an entire trail from the summit to the bottom.

At the Sugarbush Ski School, we teach the American Technique, with some of my own modifications. I still refer to our method as "delayed shoulder"—that is, the strongest part of the body, from the waist down develops the turn. As I teach it, the hips and legs initiate and enter the turn and the torso follows in a natural delayed motion. The delayed shoulder turn allows you to avoid "over-rotation." It causes slipped instead of carved turns. This delayed shoulder position is natural to the athlete. The power that it develops can be seen in all sports. Examine the pictures on these pages and you will find some interesting relationships between the movements of skiing and those of other active sports.

At this point, there is no need to be concerned about the physics involved. As you ski with me, the turn will gradually come to you. But first we must learn the basics.

Some fundamental definitions must be understood before you begin.

Fall line: the most direct route from the top to bottom of a hill. A snowball, rolling unhindered, will follow this line.

Uphill ski: the ski, naturally, on the uphill side of the mountain as you stand in a traverse position. Downhill ski: the other one.

Traverse: to ski across the fall line.

Mogul: a large mound of snow on a slope caused when a number of skiers turn in the same place and heel-kick the snow into a pile.

Similarity in position is seen in these comparison photos of Stein and a British football player. Note delayed shoulder of player as he uses twisting power to make a turn.

91

Tip: the front end of the ski. Also known as the *shovel*, which is the curved-up part. The other end of the ski is the *tail*.

Other terms will be defined as they occur in describing the maneuvers.

In most of the descriptions throughout this section of the book, I illustrate what I consider to be the basic *keys* to the successful performance of each maneuver. We do the same in our ski school and if you practice these motions until they become perfect, then the entire sequence will become easy to do.

Other athletes draw turning power from the counter-rotational twist of delayed shoulder. Note tremendous power golfers derive from this twisting movement as portrayed by Jack Nicklaus, left.

92

BASIC DOWNHILL RUNNING POSITION

HERE IS THE CORRECT RUNNING POSITION on flat ground—the same position that is taken on a slope. One ski is slightly advanced. Weight is equally distributed, ankles well bent as knees press forward. Boot of the advanced ski fits into concave portion of the other boot.

THE KEY:

Don't stick out your derrière. Bend a little forward from the waist, so that the chest is slightly advanced ahead of the knees. Poles are carried at the sides; elbows are close to the waist, with pole baskets trailing. The ankles are bent forward so much that there is pressure of the top of the boot against the front of the ankle.

POLE GRIP

Grip pole by inserting hand from below the loop until strap encircles the wrist. Then open your hand and let it fall on the strap. Then seize the handle and grip firmly.

FALLING AND RISING

Everyone falls and you should learn to relax when it happens. Try to fall safely. Never try to fall forward. If you are in trouble, simply try to sit back and to one side like a prim lady in a subway car. Don't lock your knees. Keep them bent and take the impact on your seat. After a fall, keep your skis parallel across the fall line and draw your knees to you. Remove your wrists from the pole straps and dig the poles into the snow on the uphill side of your body close to your hip. Grasp the pole with your uphill hand just above the basket. Now place the palm of your downhill hand over the butt of the pole handle. *Pull* with the *downhill* arm and *push* with the uphill arm away from the slope. You're up!

WALKING ON THE FLAT

First, assume the correct stance. Then slide the left ski forward as you move the right pole forward. Plant the right pole, pushing yourself forward from the left ski. Now slide the right ski forward and put your weight on it as you move the left pole forward. Plant the pole and push.

THE KEY:

The skis are not lifted. They are slid flat along the snow. Use the poles to give you that added momentum. Right pole forward with the left ski; left pole with the right ski.

TURNING ON THE FLAT—STEP TURN AROUND

Your skis are parallel on the flat snow, with both poles dug in at your sides for support and balance. Now lift the left ski and move it a foot to the side. Now, the right ski, and place it next to the left in parallel position again. Plant the poles. Repeat stepping movement.

THE KEY:

Use the tails of the skis as an axis. Note that the tails of the skis never move from the center. If you make a complete turn and have done this correctly, there will be a perfect fan pattern in the snow.

CLIMBING

Now we begin making our first moves on the slope. In order to learn how to ski down, we have to learn how to get up there. Here are the two basic methods:

SIDE STEP

Face across the fall line, pole tips planted at your sides. Ankles and knees are tilted uphill for edge control. Lean slightly forward, the pit of your neck in a line with the toepiece of the binding of the downhill ski. Lift poles and move your uphill ski about a foot up the slope. Dig the ski in on its uphill edge and plant both poles at your sides for support. Then step up with the downhill ski until the skis are once again together and parallel. Each time you lift your uphill ski, you lift both poles.

HERRINGBONE

Face the slope and up the fall line. Spread your ski tips about a pole length apart. Keep the tails of the skis together. Turn your ankles inward toward each other. This will prevent back-sliding by edging the skis into the snow at an angle to the fall line. Dig your pole tips in behind you; hold your elbows at your sides. Now lift your left ski and plant it a foot up the slope on its inside edge. At the same time, bring the right pole forward and plant it. Repeat by lifting and planting the right ski a foot up the slope on its inside edge and bringing your left pole forward and planting it behind you for support.

THE KEY:

It's in the edging caused by the inward turn of the ankles and knees, —and in keeping the poles slightly behind you. Some skiers make better progress if they keep their hands cupped over the butts of the poles. It helps them push.

TURNING ON A SLOPE—THE KICK TURN

Many skiers have gotten along quite well without learning the kick turn. But in an emergency situation—where you have traversed across a trail, for instance, and find you are unable to turn normally—the kick turn is the only way you can get out of it. And if you are climbing a slope in a series of traverses and want to make another, higher, traverse, only the kick turn will do. It's simple enough to learn and should be practiced.

Practice on the flat. Imagine your skis to be across the fall line. Downhill is on your right. Keep your elbows at your sides, turn your upper body downhill and dig in both pole tips behind you, about a shoulder width apart. Now, lean your body on both poles. Slide your right (downhill) ski forward in a high kick that will allow you to plant the tail of the ski into the snow beside the tip of the left (uphill) ski so that the ski is at a 90-degree angle to the snow. Now let the tip of the right ski fall downhill until it points directly opposite and parallel to the left ski. Step on your right ski with all of your weight and at the same time, swing around the left ski into the new traverse position.

THE KEY:
When you kick-turn on a hill, always turn your upper body downhill and plant your poles behind you, a shoulder width apart to begin. To feel secure lean on your poles and put all of your weight on the uphill ski.

THE FIRST RUN

Now we are ready to take our first run down a gentle slope. Begin by side-stepping up the hill, first making sure that there is a flat runout so that you will come to a natural stop. You have side-stepped to the point on the hill from which you plan to make your run. You are in a traverse position. Now you must face the fall line. Here's what you do: Dig in both pole tips below you, spaced about shoulder-width apart. Place the butts of the pole handles in the palms of your hands and lock your elbows so that there is a straight line from pole tips to shoulders. Your weight, if you do this, is supported by your bones— not by the use of your muscles. Once you are in this position, it is easy enough to step-turn the ski until they are between the tips of the poles, facing downhill. Assume the downhill running position and press forward with your knees. You're off. Let the skis slide downhill and lift the poles out of the snow as you pass them.

THE KEY:

Knees and ankles pressed forward as you run downhill; one ski slightly advanced to establish a natural running position and to avoid crossing skis as you go over uneven terrain. And when you get into position, don't forget to lock your elbows. Bend ankles forward and keep the arms relaxed alongside the body.

SNOWPLOW POSITION AND SNOWPLOW STOP

Obviously we won't always have a flat runout to bring us to a gentle halt after a downhill run. Here's where we learn our first braking (and turning) maneuver—the snow plow. It's best to learn the position first on the flat before moving to a slope.

Take the correct downhill position, then spread the tails of the skis apart about the length of a ski pole. Keep the tips slightly apart—about the width of a ski-pole basket. Your knees and ankles are bent forward. The knees point toward the tips of the skis. Your upper body is bent slightly forward from the waist. Again, don't arch your back—your rear must not stick out. The arms are in a relaxed position at the sides of your body. The inside edges of your skis are tilted slightly into the snow. This is the snowplow running position.

Now, from this position, lift your body momentarily to take the weight off the skis. This will flatten them and allow them to start sliding. Then, sink down to the original position and continue running down the fall line. In the snow plow, your body weight is distributed equally on both skis. To stop—raise up again, at the same time push both heels of your skis farther apart out to the side and tilt the upper body slightly forward.

Correct snow-plow position, left, showing proper distance between tips. Center photo shows distance between tails of skis. Illustrated directly above are some points to remember: (1) Ankles are bent forward. (2) Knees point toward tips of skis. Note relationship of ankles to skis as skis are edged. (3) Too much bending of the knees inward results in improper position.

A RUN USING THE SNOW PLOW

As you learned earlier, side step up a gentle hill and step turn into the fall line. Begin a parallel run by pressing your knees and ankles forward, one slightly ahead of the other. As you move downhill, lift up by pushing up from your skis. As the skis become unweighted (you can feel the lack of resistance), push the tails apart and sink down into the snowplow position. Remember to keep the body weight equally distributed over both skis. From the snowplow position, now unweight again, and bring the skis together, one ahead of the other. When you have mastered these moves, try climbing farther up the hill to give yourself a longer run, and practice linking the snow plow and the downhill run together.

THE KEY:

Illustration shows snow-plow section of run. In this case, I side-step into position, adjust myself into proper snow plow, then by' lifting my poles and flattening my skis slightly, I allow myself to slide downhill. Arms are in line with poles when getting into position. Body weight is equally distributed over both skis. From this position, unweight and bring skis together.

THE FIRST TURN

Remember, when you kept both skis equally weighted in the snow-plow position, you went straight ahead slowly. The speed was controlled by the pressure on your inside edges.

Now, if you weight one ski, you will slowly turn in the direction that ski is pointing. Let's say you want to turn right. Begin with a snowplow position and let yourself run for a few feet. Now, put most of your weight to your left ski by leaning over the left boot, your left shoulder dropped a little with a slight twist of your left hip downhill. You will begin moving toward the right.

Release the weight on the left ski, bring your shoulder square again so that you are in the normal snowplow position. Now shift your weight to your right ski, your right shoulder dropped slightly, upper body leaning out over your right boot. Again twist your right hip downhill slightly—and you move to the left.

You have accomplished your first turns—using the snow plow.

THE KEY:

The snowplow position remains the same at all times, but in the turn, the downhill knee is slightly more bent than the uphill knee.

DELAYED SHOULDER SNOWPLOW TURN

From the snowplow position in the fall line, twist your left shoulder and hip back with an uplift of the body. (This is the wind-up that gives you the power to bring yourself around.)

Now, press your left hip forward and down toward your left ski. The shoulder follows "delayed" or shortly behind the hip and you find yourself turning to the right. Opposite action will turn you to the left. Try linking these turns; it's the first delayed shoulder turn in your repertoire.

Diagram shows a very
simple slalom
course for practicing
linked snowplow turns.
Two ski poles spaced about
ten feet apart form
a gate. It's fun to do
and will add some
spice to your practice
sessions, besides getting
you accustomed to
weight shifting
and edge control.

107

SIDE SLIP

You have learned something about edge control while making snow-plow turns. The key to more advanced skiing is this subtle use of the edges, especially when you begin to learn what are known as "skidding turns," or "christies." Side-slipping exercises teach you edge control. Side-slipping is also useful as an emergency measure—for instance, on trails or slopes where you find it difficult to turn.

Take a position on a relatively steep slope (steeper than you have been using for snowplow exercises). Your skis are across the fall line —uphill boot, knee, hip, and shoulder about a half-boot length ahead. Your downhill knee is tucked behind your uphill knee and your knees are flexed. Your upper body faces downhill, your poles pointing behind you, parallel to each other. Now, spring upward easily, and at the same time roll your knees and ankles away from the hill. This will release the edges (flatten the skis) and you will slide sideways down the fall line. Slide a few feet down the slope, then sink down again, tilting your uphill edges into the slope by the roll of ankles and knees into the hill to stop sliding.

THE KEY:

Edging is accomplished by rolling your ankles and knees into the hill. Release the edges by rolling the knees and ankles away from the hill.

PROPER TRAVERSE POSITION—FROM THE FRONT   **FROM THE BACK**

TRAVERSING

Now that you have learned to control your edges so that you can slip sideways, you must learn how to travel across the fall line to the point where you will want to make your turn. This is known as traversing and is a part of every skiing maneuver where the skis are parallel. It's extremely important to have a proper traversing position for preparation for stem christies and parallel turns.

Face across the fall line at about 60 degrees with your skis edged uphill and boots pressed together—the convex section of your downhill boot fits into the concave instep of your uphill boot—your downhill knee tucked behind your uphill knee. Uphill shoulder and hip lead the lower body and are twisted into the hill. Your upper body leans *outward*, that is, downhill. This will put the weight where it always belongs in traversing and in parallel skiing—mainly on the downhill ski. In fact, although it seems contrary to your natural instinct, on steep slopes more outward lean of the upper body gives you more control in that it forces more weight on the downhill ski and causes your skis to become more edged. Poles are parallel in line with the skis. Your arms are bent at the elbows. Always look in the direc-

Far left, improper traverse—knees are together, but ankles and boots are not. Closeup, left, shows proper position of knees, ankles, feet, and skis.

Below, note difference between this closeup and one above. Another fault is below, right. Tips are crossed because uphill ski did not lead and weight was not on downhill ski.

tion of travel, *not* at your skis. Now push off, and remember, do not stiffen the lower leg—keep it flexed. I have found this is one of the most common mistakes skiers make. A little bounce up and down helps you balance.

TRAVERSE AND SIDE-SLIP EXERCISE

Here is where we combine what you have learned so far—side-slipping and traversing—to give you your first feel of parallel skiing.

Run in a traverse position for about twenty feet, then smoothly lift your body upward and forward toward your ski tips as you flatten both skis by releasing the edges. Now, roll the knees slightly into the hill. The tails of your skis will automatically slide downhill. Let them slide about a foot. Then, sink down again into a traverse position and roll your ankles so that the inside edges bite hard into the snow. Remember to maintain the traversing position—upper body angled downhill. Your downhill shoulder should be dropped slightly and kept back.

Any turn that involves a slide of parallel skis is a christie; you have just made one—into the hill.

INTERMEDIATE SKIING

THE SNOWPLOW CHRISTIE

YOU HAVE LEARNED ALL OF THE FUNDAMENTAL MANEUVERS OF EARLY SKIING—straight snow plow, traversing, side slip, and the snowplow turn. Now you are ready to put all of these together in what we call the "snowplow christie," which must be accomplished successfully before moving into more advanced turning maneuvers. There is great satisfaction in learning the snowplow christie, because for the first time you will be coming out of the turn with your skis parallel.

As we have seen earlier, there is a key to success in every skiing maneuver. In the snowplow christie, the key is a definite up-lift and down-sink (see the accompanying illustrations) between each segment of the maneuver. To do otherwise would mean an unsuccessful attempt to force the skis against the friction of the snow.

Photo sequence shows fall-line phase of snowplow christie. I wind up to prepare for the turn, sink down to start the turn, then cross the fall line. See following pages for complete sequence.

113

UP-LIFT   TRAVERSE

DOWN-SINK

WINDUP

DOWN-SINK

CROSS FALL LINE

UP-LIFT AND SHIFT WEIGHT   PARALLEL TRAVERSE

UP-LIFT

114

THE KEY:
It's all in knowing when to up-unweight so that the skis are not forced around. Here I demonstrate the beginning of the turn. From a traverse (1), I unweight (2), taking the pressure off both skis so that I can spread the tails into a snowplow without forcing them against the snow (3).

I begin the maneuver in a traverse, where, to review, everything uphill is advanced—ski, boot, knee, hip, arm, and even ear. (Picture 1). Next comes the second position, straight snow plow. How do I get from a traverse into the snow plow? By up-unweighting (2), the result of taking pressure off both skis at once (see inset photos) so that I can push the tails of both skis out.

Then, (5), I wind up to begin preparing for the turn, sink down to start the turn (6), and cross the fall line (7). Now, something new —with an up-lift (8), I transfer all of my weight to the downhill ski. The uphill ski, with no pressure on it, can easily be moved parallel to the downhill ski.

Now, traverse with a slight down-sink and you are on the way toward parallel skiing.

THE STEM CHRISTIE

THE FIRST REAL CARVING TURN in your repertoire is the stem christie. When you have accomplished the stem christie and can do it well, then you are ready to make that big trip to the top of the mountain. With a good stem christie a skier can ski most conditions and most terrain; to have reached the stem christie stage is to have reached another plateau of learning.

I prefer the uphill stem that is used in the American Technique, because when you push your upper ski into position, you are pushing it in the direction in which you want to turn. As a result, you can get into and out of the fall line more quickly.

When you want to try your first stem christies, choose an area that is free of moguls or other terrain variations. Otherwise they will occupy your mind; you must be completely free to concentrate on the movements of the turn so that theory becomes a reality.

1

2

3

THE KEY:
The position of the hip at the moment when I bring the skis together is most important. The hip must be held back slightly during the fall line phase of the turn. I accomplish this by holding my downhill or inside arm back, as in figure 1, 2, and 3. Otherwise your skis will tend to slide instead of carve the turn. Actually what you are doing is automatically putting more weight on the downhill ski to help you carve the turn. Again, remember to drop the downhill shoulder in the turn.

PREPARATION

TRAVERSE

INITIATION

Downhill ski is always in a straight line.

FALL LINE

COMPLETION

118

Proper traverse position is always important before you begin any turn. If you are not in a proper starting position to begin with, you can be sure that the turn will not be proper. To start the stem christie, your body should be directly over your skis. Don't hang forward in your bindings so that all of the pressure is on the tips of the skis. Your weight should be mainly over the downhill ski as in the first picture of the sequence photos.

At the preparation for the turn, I plant my downhill pole and sink on my downhill ski with all of my weight, to enable me to put the uphill ski in a stem position. This stemmed ski is now nearly in line with the fall line.

To initiate the turn, I push off from the heavily weighted ski—the downhill ski—and transfer the weight to the uphill ski (the downhill ski of the new turn).

At the moment the weight transfer takes place, the skis begin to come together. Pay close attention to the position of the hip at this point. It must not come around too much or too soon. If it does, your skis will tend to slide instead of carve.

How do I prevent this from happening? In the sequence photos, look at my downhill arm as I near the end of the fall line phase of the turn. See how I hold it back slightly. That is what you should do. I find that anything I do with my arm and shoulder I tend to do with my hip. When I throw a ball, for instance, at the moment the ball leaves the hand, both the shoulder and hip move together. So, when I hold back my arm and shoulder in skiing, I also hold back my hip.

During the completion phase of the turn, I gradually come around, feeding the turn little by little by letting the hip come around slowly with the arm delayed.

Gradually, I reach a normal traverse position during the completion phase of the turn. I am now ready to prepare for another stem christie.

THE PARALLEL CHRISTIE

Not until you have learned the parallel turn can you consider
yourself a complete skier. Yet many skiers reach the stem christie stage
and go no further; they complain that the parallel christie is very difficult for them to learn.

I have often wondered why this is so. I think the secret is in the
proper setting of a "platform" before going into the turn, something
that takes practice and understanding, but will, in the end, make a
parallel skier out of anyone marooned on the stem christie plateau.
A platform is when your weight is equally distributed on both skis
with a maximum simultaneous edge set.

I had always been able to ski parallel before I came to the United
States, but I was never sure what the term meant until the season of
1953 when I taught in Sun Valley. I was allowed to teach pupils to
ski the way I did, which was not the accepted book method at the
time. But it *was* based on my racing experience. I taught a method of
learning how to ski parallel that was similar to the new "delayed
shoulder" technique that was soon introduced.

Very little has been changed since that time, although teaching
techniques have undergone constant revision in attempts to aid the
pupil in learning the more difficult phases of skiing. No two people,
however, ski alike—as anyone watching downhill trails from a lift
will recognize. So, in my teaching, I attempt to concentrate on certain
salient points that make learning much easier.

In learning to ski parallel, most important is understanding how to
set a platform in that precise moment before starting your turn.

Following your traverse, the weight must be evenly distributed on
both skis—fifty percent on the uphill ski and fifty percent on the
downhill. At this moment, *and for a split second only*, my body is in a
crouch—the only time it is in this position during the entire turn. I
stress *split second* because if I remain in this position too long, I will
not be able to develop the bounce that is absolutely essential and I will
start turning into the hill.

Another secret. Look at the sixth picture in the turn sequence.
Notice that I have already started to advance my *downhill* ski before
my skis are in the fall line. This ski becomes the uphill ski when I
advance through the turn.

What happens if I do not advance my downhill ski at this moment?
The change of body position from traverse to a turning position forces
the skis apart unless they change position with the body.

Some people have difficulty, when they traverse, in keeping their
skis parallel and together. Sometimes their knees are together, but
their skis are apart. Why does this happen? Look at your skis when
you find yourself not traversing properly. You probably will find that
the uphill ski is flat on the snow while the other ski is edged.

Another secret, therefore: Make sure that both skis have the same angle in the snow. In the traverse (as opposed to your platform), put most of the weight on the downhill ski, the knees together, the skis edged equally, and they will run together.

Now, let's run through a turn. The traversing and fall line phases are shown on these pages. Examine them carefully.

Start out in a perfect traverse position. Now prepare for the important platform with a slight lift of the body. Then sink into the platform with a push of the heels downhill (heel thrust), for a brief second. Notice, in the sequence photos how my body position changes, the edges of my skis having, at this point, the maximum angle with the snow. Then, a slight bounce, or heel thrust uphill. At this precise moment, my downhill ski begins to come forward and becomes the uphill ski after the turn has been completed.

Some points on which to concentrate:

The body remains in a slight reverse position with the turn and stays in that position until the traverse position is reached again.

The longer you can keep the reverse, or delayed shoulder, position with your body, the longer you will be able to carve the turn.

Try to feel your edges and *ski* on them. This gives complete control from the start and avoids the terrible feeling of the skis not holding.

Do not force your weight forward over your toes. Notice, in the photos, that I do not sit back on my heels either. My weight is distributed over the entire foot. Of course, there is more weight on the downhill ski than on the uphill ski on an average steep hill and in good snow conditions. *Under icy conditions* about seventy percent of the weight should be on the downhill ski—with more outward lean than is normal.

TRAVERSE

SLIGHT LIFT

LIFT

SINK INTO PLATFORM

HEEL THRUST WITH SLIGHT LIFT

THE KEY:

Sequence photos show only the traverse, platform, and fall line phases of the turn because these are the most important sections of it. I begin in a perfect traversing position, top photo, then I prepare to go into the platform with a slight lift of the body. Then I sink, make a platform by weighting equally on both skis for a fraction of a second. Then, a slight bounce, or uphill heel thrust, at which point my downhill ski comes forward. (Uphill heel thrust amounts to a changing of the edges.) My body remains slightly reversed. As the turn continues, I hold my position until I begin traversing again to prepare for the next turn.

The inset photos illustrate the key to successful parallel turns: lift, sink into platform, heel thrust—and into the fall line. A common mistake: the lack of uphill heel thrust. This results in the skier landing on a flat ski instead of an edged ski. The skier may then catch an outside edge—the worst enemy of parallel skiing.

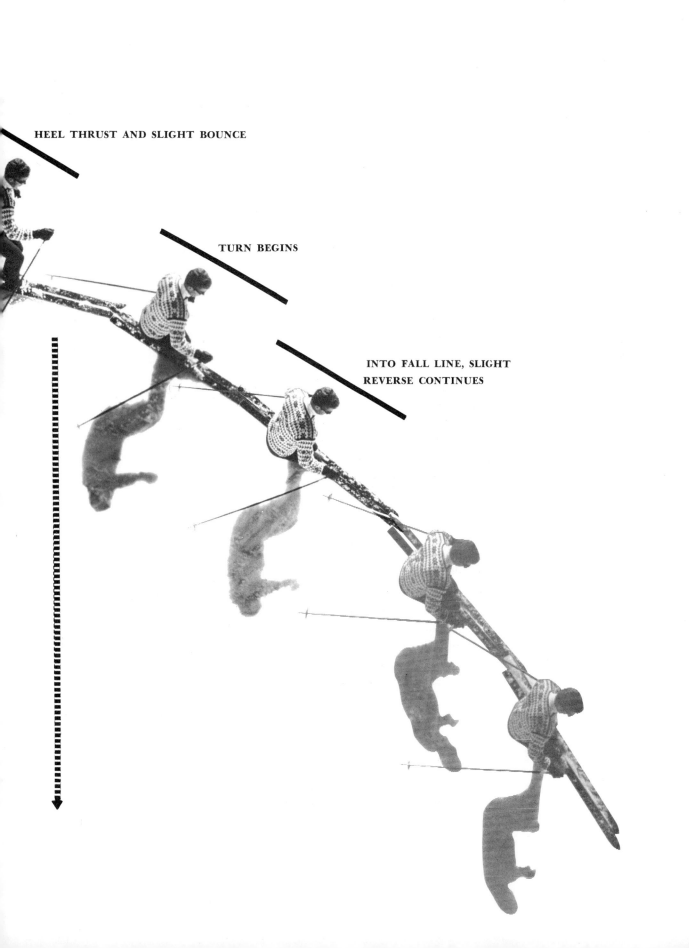

HEEL THRUST AND SLIGHT BOUNCE

TURN BEGINS

INTO FALL LINE, SLIGHT
REVERSE CONTINUES

ADVANCED SKIING

THE MARK OF A GOOD SKIER is his ability to make a smoothly-carved, graceful parallel turn. The parallel turn, as I have demonstrated it on the previous pages, is essentially a long-radius christie. It works best on relatively open slopes or wide trails under any sort of snow conditions. With a good long-radius christie there is very little that he will be unable to ski.

But often the skier encounters conditions that he would like to handle with less trouble—narrow, relatively gradual trails, steep trails, moguls, high-sided bowls. The good skier is separated from the really advanced.skier by the latter's ability to handle any sort of conditions from the top to the bottom of the mountain. The advanced skier goes at a good clip taking anything that comes along in his stride.

How does he do this? Besides being at home on his skis (which comes from practice) he has other turns at his command besides the long-radius christie. In this section we'll discuss some of these turns and learn how I counter the various types of terrain and snow conditions. At the end, a few treats: the secrets of my mambo, jump, and flip.

WEDELN

FOR SKIING NARROW, MEDIUM-STEEP TRAILS, or for skiing down the fall line on a medium-steep slope where the snow is relatively well-packed, the advanced skier uses *wedeln*. Essentially, wedeln is a short-radius christie without traversing. It is a series of consecutive turns down the fall line with more frequent changing of the edges than in a delayed-shoulder parallel turn. Done properly, wedeln is a snake-like flow of motion—a dance on skis.

To wedel properly, however, always under control, is very difficult. The skier does not turn directly across the fall line as he does in a longer radius christie. Now he is plunging directly down the fall line. He must be able to control his speed. He must shift his weight almost imperceptibly. He must use heel push in order to set a platform for each change in downhill direction, but this too must be done quickly

124

and imperceptibly. Finally, he must understand that all of the work in wedeln is done by the lower body while the upper body faces downhill.

Most skiers have seen someone coming down a trail doing what is thought to be wedeln. But the difference between real wedeln and the imitation is easily apparent. He bounces up and down, waves his arms, but he is not turning. This skier's hips do not change position from one side to the other each time his knees are bent and his body is down. Wedeln must be effortless and it must keep the skier in control.

In teaching wedeln, I use an exercise that is very effective because its movements are identical with those used in wedeln. It starts with that old standby—the snowplow.

SNOWPLOW WEDELN

To start, I pick out a smooth run that is not too steep, about fifty feet long, and about four times as wide as my skis are long.

1. Starting position. My skis are in the traditional snowplow so that I can control my speed in the fall line. I lift my right arm, keeping my elbow close to the body, the palm of my hand facing downhill.

2. I twist my right hip slightly downhill, and with a drop of my right shoulder, I plant the right pole into the snow. There is no fixed place to plant the pole; it should touch the snow comfortably with the elbow close to the body.

3. My turn begins to the left. Unweighting begins.

4. The starting position is approached again and my poles begin to change position. In wedeln, only one pole should be seen at a time.

5. My left pole comes forward, right pole back. Heel thrust on left ski.

6. My left hip twists downhill. By dropping the left shoulder, I develop a snowplow wedeln turn to the right. The turn continues as shown in the remainder of the photo sequence.

Some points to remember:

The shoulders do not move forward, but remain square, facing downhill. A slight *drop* of the downhill shoulder makes it easier to execute the turn.

I never lift my arms, but keep the elbows close to my body. Lifting the arms might throw me off balance.

Once the snowplow wedeln exercise is mastered, gradually narrow the "V" of the snowplow. You will finally reach the parallel position with your skis. Facing down the fall line you will be able to perform wedeln properly—because you have learned these fundamentals.

126

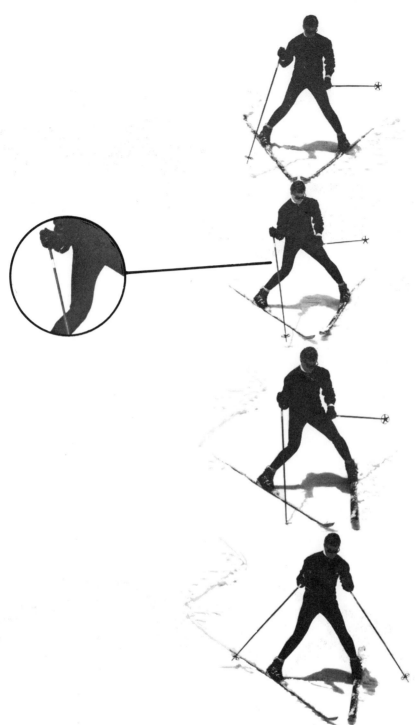

THE KEY:
I twist my hip and sink down, causing skis to begin turning.
I set my pole and establish a platform. Pole is planted comfortably
when the elbow is held into the side. Pole length determines where
point will touch snow.
I change my poles. Only one pole is seen at a time. Poles come
alongside the body. Quick action is essential for proper wedeln.
I turn in the other direction repeating the cycle.

WEDELN

SNOWPLOW WEDELN

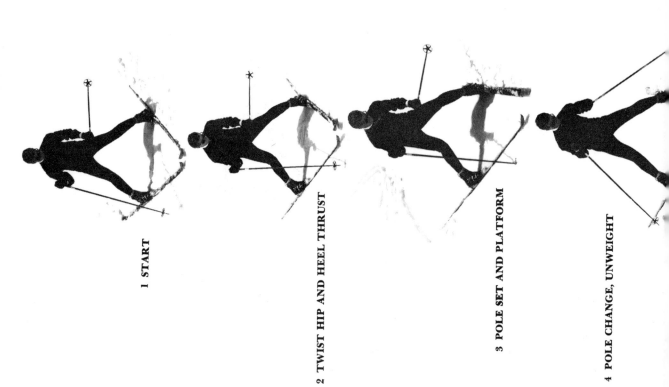

1 START

2 TWIST HIP AND HEEL THRUST

3 POLE SET AND PLATFORM

4 POLE CHANGE, UNWEIGHT

128

On the right is a
complete wedeln
sequence with the
skis parallel.
Compare it with the
snowplow wedeln
sequence and note
the same emphasis in
the movements of my
hips and legs,
the square position
of the shoulders,
and the setting
of the poles.
Note how the poles
move alongside my
body in a pendulum
motion whenever
my body is lifted
up from the skis.

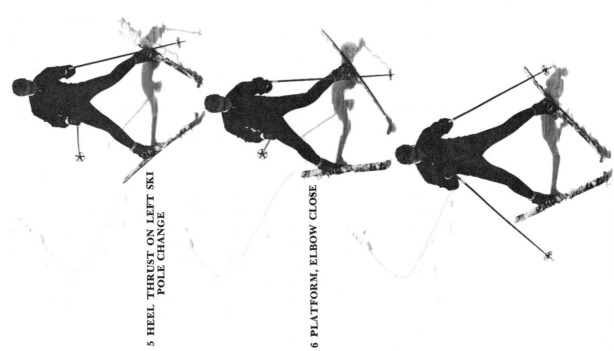

**5 HEEL THRUST ON LEFT SKI
POLE CHANGE**

6 PLATFORM, ELBOW CLOSE

7 POLE CHANGE, UNWEIGHT

129

JUMP WEDELN

As we have seen, wedeln is most useful in skiing the fall line on slopes and narrow trails that are gradual to medium steep. But what about those really steep trails that are comparatively narrow? Or crusty, breakable snow? Wedeln is not useful on them because unless you are an exceptionally able skier, you will certainly go out of control.

Most skiers tend to shy away from this sort of situation and cling to the more gradual hills or the trails where there is sufficient room to traverse and turn in the traditional long-radius christie. Even the skier who is advanced enough to wedel gracefully may avoid steep slopes; one look, and he is sure that he can't handle them.

Remember my point about being able to ski every possible type of terrain? The ability to ski steep slopes is another mark of the advanced skier. For once accomplished, everything else on the mountain becomes relatively easy.

Another point. Many skiers talk of having "bad days" when nothing seems to work for them. The way to insure not having "bad days" on skis is to ski steep runs often. The only method that works well on steep runs is the *jump wedeln*.

In jump wedeln, there is a pronounced edge set (or platform set) from which the tails of the skis are lifted in a short arc into the fall line. Poles must be used rythmically because they help give you the needed lift and quick heel thrust that are the distinguishing features of jump wedeln.

In jump wedeln, the weight remains mainly on both skis. The end of one turn is the start of the other.

Let's do the jump wedeln.

I start from a steep traverse with my downhill pole forward. I sink down, mark my turn with the downhill pole. My elbow is in toward my hip, the palm of my hand faces downhill. This is the platform. I lift from the platform by retracting my lower legs to get the tails of my skis in the air and thrust them uphill across the fall line in a short arc to the opposite position—dropping my body into a sharp comma (or extreme reverse position). I edge the skis hard, plant the new downhill pole, and lift again from the new platform.

Points to remember:

If you have equal weight on both skis as you spring from the platform, they will not split apart into a stem.

Pay attention to the position of the hip. The hip is dropped to the inside at the end of the turn so that the angle between the snow and the lower legs is about 45 degrees. This will help you ram your edges into the snow to stop the turn and establish the platform.

As in any wedeln maneuver, the poles must move rythmically with a pendulum motion alongside the body. As soon as one pole is planted, the other starts moving forward. But my rule still applies: only one pole in front of you at a time.

**POLE WORK
IN
JUMP WEDELN**

*Starting from a traverse
I am about to plant
my pole to trigger
the all-important jump
of the ski tails
off the snow. My
elbows are out from
the body, but my
poles swing close
to the legs.*

*I set the pole into
the snow by suddenly
dropping into a
crouch. I set my edges
to give me a platform
from which to make
the lift-off. I lock
my arm so that the
recoil thrust of the
pole tends to lift me
off the snow. I ski
"over the pole."*

*Springing from the
crouch, I leap
aided by the thrust
of the planted pole
against the hand.
My weight has been
equalized so that as
I spring clear, both
skis come off the
snow together, skis
parallel. My other
pole begins swinging
forward so that it
is in position for
the next turn.*

THE KEY:
All-important is establishing a solid edge set and platform from which to make the turn. It is this platform that helps you control your speed on steep slopes because you are, in fact, checking hard on each turn. After lift-off (1) I pull my ski tails in the air and swing them in a short arc across the fall line. (2) I land in the exact opposite position as I drop my body into a comma. I drop lower (3), edging the skis hard, and plant my pole. I spring up (4) from the platform and start swinging them again across the fall line.

MOGULS ARE NOT A MENACE

To SOME SKIERS, MOGULS—THOSE HILLOCKS OF SNOW caused by heel-pushing turns—are dreadful. Other skiers just flow through them—naturally and rythmically. A heavily mogulled slope, especially if it is steep, seems to set up an anxiety block in skiers who otherwise are absolutely in control. Why the panic? To me the answer is obvious; uncertainty causes the skier to forget almost everything he knows.

There is no reason to be uncertain in a field of moguls. Like every-thing else in skiing, there are secrets to skiing this type of terrain. But the secrets are based on sound fundamentals. Once you adapt them to a mogulled slope you'll never be uncertain again. You'll consider moguls a challenge, seek them out, and ski them with relaxed aban-don. Face it, they're here to stay. Despite the use of over-the-snow mogul-cutting machinery, one day's hard skiing on steep slopes with new snow will set those moguls up again.

Deep moguls have been as much of a challenge to me as to anyone else. I have been in serious trouble in them. In 1955, taking the Canyon Run at Sun Valley, I ran into a mogul patch at high speed. I was sure, on this day, that I could handle them as easily as I had the day before. Twenty-four hours earlier, I had skimmed over their tops and in and around them, flexing my knees at just the right moments. Everything about the run had been exhilarating: a rythmic, quick dance.

But on this day I was tired. My concentration and judgement were slightly off. One mogul threw me off balance. I flew through the air for about sixty feet and landed on another mogul. I must have been traveling at least fifty miles an hour and when I hit, I heard my leg snap at the moment of impact.

The result was a compound fracture. While recuperating I reflected on the nature of mogul skiing and decided that since it involved spe-cial problems there should be a clear method for doing it properly.

134

Let's start with the analysis of a common mistake and refer to the accompanying illustrations.

Most skiers turn too late. In the sequence photo, note that my right pole (2) is planted in the snow about a foot ahead of the ridge of the mogul. This spot is my turning point—clearly shown in photo 4 where the turn has been started just as the boots pass the pole basket.

Why do I plant the pole at this spot—a foot in front of the ridge? Because, when I turn at this spot, I am able to ski down the other (downhill) side of the mogul, finish the turn in the hollow (5, 6), and prepare for the next turn. On the way up (11), I plant my pole ahead of the following ridge (12), and repeat the turn cycle again.

Note that as I pass the spot where my pole has been planted (4), the heels of the skis are lifted off the snow and the tips of the skis are dropped (5). Essentially this is a *pre-jump*, a move you make to keep the mogul from throwing you into the air. It's done by tucking your feet under your thighs rather than by straightening your upper body. If by lifting your upper half you attempt to lift your skis off the snow, it will take too long to return to the proper position again

and you will lose the most important element of mogul-skiing—the rhythm.

Some points to remember:

As in wedeln, all the action is from the waist down; my legs operate like springs, coiling and uncoiling. Any stiffness in the knees will throw you off.

When it is very steep I lift my uphill ski so that my weight is placed automatically where it should be—on the downhill ski.

The pole change must be quick, in a pendulum action alongside the body. One pole replaces the other as you prepare for the next turn. If your pole isn't ready to hit that spot one foot ahead of the mogul ridge, your rhythm will be destroyed. When your rhythm is off, it's better to stop completely and then start again and try to retain the smooth motion.

*Know where you're going
before you get there.
Pick the mogul
around which you want
to turn and plant your pole
early. On steep slopes,
I lift the heel of my
inside ski to make sure the
outside ski gets plenty of
weight. I leave both skis
on the snow on more gentle slopes.*

MORE MOGUL TIPS

In practicing your mogul technique, whether you are an intermediate or advanced skier, try starting at the bottom. That is, climb up from the bottom of the slope and run several moguls until you are satisfied with your progress. Then, climb higher and higher for each run.

On your first run down a mogulled slope, don't go alone. Ski with someone you trust implicitly, so that you are not tense. Don't stiffen your knees; bounce. And ski two or three moguls at a time so that you can develop a proper rhythm.

MOGULS FOR INTERMEDIATES

You don't have to be an advanced skier in order to handle a bumpy slope. Intermediates who haven't reached the parallel stage often are faced with a mogul-filled slope that they would like to tackle. There's no reason why they shouldn't. Here's what to do to make your turns if you're still using a stem christie.

Approach the mogul from an angle and head, at a moderate speed, toward the uprise of the mogul. Plant your pole about a foot ahead of the ridge and prepare for your turn as you would in a normal stem christie. Place your uphill ski into a half-snowplow position, and transfer your weight to it from the downhill ski. Right after you pass the ridge, your skis will have closed. Turn around the planted pole, sliding down the down-side of the mogul in a side slip.

Adjust your side slip to the terrain. The steeper the terrain, the longer the side slip. Aim your skis as you come out of the side slip into a traverse toward the uprise of the next mogul and repeat the maneuver.

Again, pole plant is essential. Get the tip into the snow about a foot ahead of the ridge and mark your turn there, not only to control your speed, but also to help you pick up the rhythm.

SECRETS OF THE STEIN TURN

Although the trademark of my skiing—the extreme reverse shoulder turn—was developed because of the requirements of slalom racing, it wasn't until I came to Sun Valley in the early fifties at the age of twenty-six that I began to perfect it.

The nurturing ground of the Stein turn was the terrain of those incredible Sun Valley bowls—Christmas, Easter, Left, Mayday, and the others. Here are high, sweeping walls, plunges unbroken by trees, all funnelling into high-sided gullies.

Bowl skiing done well gives you a tremendous feeling of speed and graceful soaring. The secret is to allow the physical forces of your speed to help carry you up the side walls. Instead of fighting gravity

and centrifugal force, you enlist them. The easiest way to learn the reverse shoulder turn as I perform it is to practice it in a bowl or on a high-sided trail—a *piste* that is essentially U-shaped in profile.

Most important: get your body weight to the inside of the turn, and at the same time keep your legs at a low angle so that you can jam the edges into the snow. The faster the speed, the closer the legs should be to the snow. The lower-body lean toward the inside gives you a hard-driving, perfectly-controlled high-speed turn. The upper body is reversed—it bends toward the outside of the turn. The lower body position—in toward the wall—helps you carve the turn without slipping. This is the Stein turn, and once you are able to do it well by the use of bowl or gully skiing, you will be able to transfer it to other slopes.

Let's do it.

I am in a fast traverse on the floor of a bowl between two walls. As soon as I begin to climb the wall, I *start my turn*; I do not wait until the apex of the wall has been reached. First, a slight check that puts the weight evenly on both skis. From this platform, I lift up slightly and as I come down again I put my weight on the *outside* ski. But I do this gradually, so that the turn will stretch out.

Now, into a reverse position to help power the turn: outside hip and shoulder back as extreme as the angle of the wall will allow. (The steeper the wall, the more extreme is the reverse.)

It seems impossible, but the weight is on my outside ski from the time I sink down until the very end of the turn. The more speed I have, the more I lean inward and the less likely it seems that I have my weight on the outside ski—but it is true. Centrifugal force helps me; it presses my weight firmly on that ski.

As the turn progresses, my body slowly comes around to lead the turn. Then, as I come off the wall, I begin squaring my position and I slowly straighten my legs. But not too early. My hip does not become square until I prepare my next turn.

In practicing this turn, let yourself go. It works best at high speed. Relax—ski with abandon. Once experienced, the sensation of a high-speed reverse shoulder turn is unforgettable.

<u>Some points to remember:</u>

Approach the wall of the bowl or gully at a 45-degree angle across the fall line. If you traverse directly across the fall line (90 degrees) it becomes almost impossible to make a proper turn. If your angle of attack is less than 45 degrees (closer to the fall line) then you reduce the enjoyment of using the banks to make the turn.

The more speed, the less heel thrust. But do not forget to set the platform from which the takeoff is made. The weight must be on *both* skis. If the weight is unevenly distributed you will be forced into a stem christie and lose the enjoyment of the long carving turn.

Maximum angulation comes at the apex of the turn.

Pole plant: It's done at the platform. The *outside* arm is back holding the *uphill* pole. Then the movement is carried through so that the maximum reverse is reached at the apex.

If you have done everything right after reaching the apex of the turn, you will automatically be swinging in the other direction. The perfect termination of the turn is when you automatically find yourself in the proper starting position for the next turn. As you cross the gully you set yourself up for the other bank by a quick edge change and body reverse.

The faster the speed, the sooner you can start the new turn and the lower on the bank you can begin it. Here is where centrifugal force is working for you. You must have maximum momentum. Otherwise you will not reach a point that is high enough to swing you in the other direction.

COME MAMBO WITH ME

THE MAMBO IS A SWINGING TURN—and not just in a literal sense. It's the turn that adds style to your skiing. It loosens you up, gives you rhythm, and adds zest to your day on the mountain.

Personally, I love to mambo. It refines my sense of balance and keeps my timing sharp. All of the grace of the dance is carried to the slopes. In doing the mambo well I feel as ecstatic as I do in executing a perfect high-speed reverse shoulder turn.

What does it take to mambo? Balance, practice, and enthusiasm. If you go at it correctly, you will probably fall more than once. If you don't fall, you probably are not putting enough into it.

The sequence is: Run, sink, rise, swing, twist, stop (block), then repeat to the opposite side.

Shall we mambo?

THE MAMBO TURN

My skis point in the fall line.

I run in the fall line.

I sink, prepared to rise.

| *Hand further back.*

I over-rotate.

My arm, shoulder, hip, block.

I start the skis down the fall line to get up some speed. Then I *sink* by going into a half-crouch. The skis are running flat in the fall line.

I *rise* with a quick unweighting movement. At the same time, I begin *swinging* the arm leading the turn up and across my skis, turning my upper body with it. My hips *twist* in the same direction as the upper body. My skis still are flat and in the fall line. As I unweight completely, my hips and upper body have twisted as far as they will go; the *blocking* of this twist begins transmitting momentum to the heels of the skis and they start to turn in the same direction. They are still flat, and because of it they start to swing out of the fall line in response to the movement of my upper body.

As the skis begin to swing, I edge them and begin pulling my hand and arm back, then the hips and torso, until I reach my starting position. My other hand and arm automatically swing forward and across the skis and I begin my new turn with an uplift and over-rotation in the opposite direction. When reaching the climax of the over-rotation the

I rise, start to twist.	Skis in fall line, hips twist.	My shoulder, hip arm stop.	My skis turn out of fall line.	I reverse, hand back.

Blocking turns skis.	I continue reversing.	I sink to prepare for next turn.	My reverse continues.	I hold turn into fall line.

changing of the edges takes place. My skis start to change direction.

Some points to remember:

Always flatten the skis at the moment you rise to the most erect position for a split second before edge change. As you are traversing during the turn, this is not difficult. You will almost feel the point where the skis should be flat.

You must *sink* before you rise. Otherwise the skis will not turn when the momentum of the twisting movement is transmitted to them as they will not be unweighted properly. Just lifting the upper body will not do it.

Always begin in the fall line so that you will have enough speed to develop the swing-swing-swing rhythm of the mambo.

The key to the mambo is the over-rotation of the arm and shoulder driven forward by the hand. They must cross the skis as far as they can go before stopping.

In practicing the mambo, pick a medium-steep but smooth slope free from terrain variations. The more packed the slope is, the better.

COME JUMP WITH ME

JUMPING IS OF LITTLE PRACTICAL VALUE TO THE RECREATIONAL SKIER, although it is a functional asset to the downhill racer. But jumping adds spice to skiing and like the mambo it builds control and balance. Most parallel skiers jump; they come off a slight rise, let the skis take them through the air for a few feet and down they come. But it's more fun to jump deliberately, off a mogul, a bump, a ridge, or when you're good at it, a cornice.

The sequence in jumping is simple: sink, plant your poles, spring, tuck, hold the tuck, stretch, touch down, sink into a crouch.

Let's try it.

I approach the takeoff (at first a medium-sized bump or mogul) bent at the knees and coiled like a spring at the hips. As I sink into the coiled position, I swing my poles forward and plant them in the exact spot from which I plan to take off.

Depending upon my speed I jump up and forward, past my poles. I stress speed because if I am going fast, it's not necessary for me to push with my poles. I uncoil *before* I reach the top of the bump— less than a second before I think I should be jumping.

As I take off, I tuck my heels under my hips. Doing this helps my ski position; my boot toes, and therefore my ski tips, are pointed downhill parallel with the slope. I stay tucked, keeping my poles as low as I can. As I approach the landing spot I *stretch*—that is, my hands go up and my feet come down so that when I land I am almost completely uncoiled. This gives me enough bounce in my knees to absorb the shock of landing. The moment I touch down I crouch; my landing is soft.

Some points to remember about jumping:

Spring earlier than you think you should. Your body should not be "behind" your skis, which is what will happen if you take off too late. The point is to use the uprise of the bump or crest and not let it use you.

Bring the heels of your boots up sharply; force yourself to tuck them under your hips. If not, you will land ski tail first and your tail second.

When you land, drop quickly. Otherwise the shock of the landing will jar you.

COME FLIP WITH ME

THE FLIP IS FOR THE ADVENTUROUS. It is acrobatics on skis—providing the same thrill one gets in performing a perfect somersault or a half-gainer off a diving board. The feeling is one of exhilaration, of weightless spinning through the air.

I have been doing the flip for more than twenty years and each time I do it there is as much of a thrill in it for me as there is for the spectators. Strangely enough, the flip was born in wartime—during those years in which we were forbidden by the Germans to compete against each other in slalom. It was invented because we were young and fearless and needed a substitute for the challenge of racing.

Before the war, three Norwegians, Tomm Murstad, Birger Ruud, and Sverre Kolterud, had thrilled the great crowds that came out to watch the jumping contests by somersaulting during their leaps. Crazy as we were, we thought we could emulate them. But we decided to go them one better and flip off a bump in the snow. This is more dangerous since there is less height in which to make a mistake. But we didn't care.

We waited for the right moment and found it one day when the old Ródkleiva slalom hill was covered with three feet of new powder snow. We built a jump with a tremendous lip on it and piled more soft snow on the landing area. The most that could happen to us, we felt, was to go head first into the deep snow at which time there would be enough of us around to pull the unlucky one out by his heels.

I was the first one to try—and I was the unlucky one.

I knew that I had to jump up and forward from the takeoff point. This was all I knew as I picked up speed toward the lip of the bump. The lip threw me up into the air, but as I swung my head down I had the unfamiliar sensation of not knowing what had happened to the rest of my body. So I stiffened without somersaulting and made a perfect dive, straight down into the snow. I was buried up to my waist, but when they pulled me out, I was laughing. It was like the first time I had gone off one of the big jumps as a child; I had dared to do it and nothing gave me as much satisfaction as knowing I had conquered my inner fear.

The next time down I was more confident. I somersaulted and gradually with practice that day I was able to land in a sitting position. We were all able to do it, in fact. We were soaking wet—but it was wonderful.

The more we practiced, the more we realized that a long, high arc was necessary. This we attained by speeding up our inrun. Our satisfaction increased as we built up more and more speed and gained

THE STEIN FLIP

A strong sense of feel, based on years of experience, enable me to know when to begin my tuck after I hold the swan position (photos 3, 4, 5). Another secret of mine: my eyes are always open so that I am constantly aware of my position in the air.

more momentum at the lip of the jump. Finally, on one of the last attempts, I somersaulted completely and landed on my skis. I was exhausted, as we all were, but the day ended with the knowledge that we had gained another accomplishment: we had done something few had ever attempted successfully before.

Our first somersaults were done with the body in a tucked position all the way around until we landed. Later I developed the flip with a "layout" or extension of the body during mid-flight. And I added a swan-dive position at the beginning.

The stretched-out flip is easier for me because I can see where I am at all times. After taking off, I hold the layout until I reach the top of the arc. The feeling can only be described as the one an eagle must feel as he soars—completely free. I am weightless at the top of the arc just before I tuck to begin the somersault that puts me right side up again.

After the flip, I stretch out in a standing position, my arms out,

154

and prepare for the landing. The skis hit the snow, I crouch as I would in a normal jump, the flip has ended, and I have done a forward somersault on skis.

If you would like to attempt the flip, examine the accompanying photos and their captions carefully. It takes courage to try it the first time and I would suggest that you do as we did during those war years in Norway—make sure that there is plenty of soft snow in the landing area. Speed is very important during the inrun so that you can gain maximum height and arc.

Why flip on skis? For the same reason, perhaps, that jumpers leap off big hills and fly several hundred feet through the air. There are smaller jumping hills; why not be content with those?

With me the flip is another challenge—another way in which I can define the limits of my being. For some there is a constant striving toward something that, in the end, may be unattainable. If you are like that, a seeker of new experiences on skis, then come flip with me.

QUESTIONS SKIERS ASK

BEGINNERS AND INTERMEDIATES ASK:

Q. *How do I get my uphill ski advanced without having to think about it?*
A. If you tuck your downhill knee up and behind the uphill knee, your uphill ski will automatically be advanced.

Q. *How do I keep my weight on the downhill ski throughout the turn?*
A. You do it by dropping your downhill shoulder. Lift the shoulder and you take the weight off the downhill ski.

Q. *How do I carve a turn?*
A. You will *carve* your turn instead of *slipping*, if you keep your downhill shoulder back and your body angulated. If, in the turn, your downhill shoulder comes around too far and too fast, you will pull the hip with you, also you will over-rotate and side slip instead of carve.

Q. *Advanced skiers ask:*
A. How do I keep the ski tips up on the surface in powder snow?
You sit back on the skis to release the pressure on the tips; the feeling is almost one of aquaplaning or water-skiing. Use your thigh muscles to help bring up the tips.

Q. *How do I pick a line?*
A. Through moguls, the easiest line to ski is the fall line. If you use the points I outlined in this section, you will be less fatigued if you "river-run" through the moguls instead of traversing across them. If possible, pick a route where the skis will turn on flat surfaces. The sides of a trail are usually easier to ski than the center. The best track is not where most of the other skiers obviously have been. Be aware of all of the possibilities of the run and keep looking ahead for your next turning point.

Q. *Besides constant practice, how can I improve my skiing?*
A. Try not to stop too frequently. Stop only if your rhythm is off, or if you feel out of control. Otherwise, keep going. You'll find, if you do this, your rhythm will improve, your skiing will improve, and you'll enjoy your day on the slopes more.

GENERAL QUESTIONS I AM ASKED:

Q. *How can I ski well when the light is flat?*
A. I wish I knew. The best advice is to ski on trails you know well and slow down. Keep loose so that you are not surprised by bumps you are unable to see. Wear goggles with amber or yellow lenses. They

sharpen definition of the bumps. And if possible stay off slopes where there are no trees for orientation.

Q. *How can I ski all day without getting tired?*
A. Providing your physical condition is good, rhythmic deep breathing while you ski will cut down fatigue. A good trick is to force yourself to exhale loudly as racers do. I often carry a little concentrated grape sugar with me for extra energy if I know that I am planning to ski all day.

Q. *How can I hold on hard-packed snow better than my friends do?*
A. Keep your edges sharp and free of burrs. If you don't feel qualified to sharpen the edges yourself, have your ski shop do it regularly. Burrs and nicks may occur after a day's skiing and can throw you off. A simple pocket hone lightly passed over the edges will eliminate them.

Q. *How should I mount my bindings?*
A. For recreational skiing, the ball of the big toe should be on the middle of the running surface of the ski. The running surface can be found by pressing the skis together so that no light shows between them. From the tails to where they part at the tips is the running surface. This is my own formula. I've used it for racing and for free skiing and it works.

Q. *How do I conquer fear of speed?*
A. Ski with someone who skis slightly faster than you do. Follow him as closely as you can and do everything he does. After a few runs you'll find that your speed has increased without your being aware of it.

Q. *How should I introduce my children to skiing?*
A. Take them with you on a skiing trip, but don't force them to ski. Let them watch others. After a while they will probably wish to start on their own. If they're very young, make sure that they are dressed warmly. Children are naturally competitive; they'll discover the fun of skiing for themselves provided they are given the opportunity to do so.

Q. *How do I avoid being disappointed with my skiing progress?*
A. Be patient. It took you two years to learn to walk. You cannot learn to ski in a day. Each plateau is an accomplishment in itself.

Q. *How can I get my wife interested in skiing?*
A. Take a week's ski vacation alone. Have a picture taken with a good-looking instructress. Then send it home. If it doesn't work, continue skiing alone. It's too much fun to give up.

What I have learned
is that
skiing is beauty...

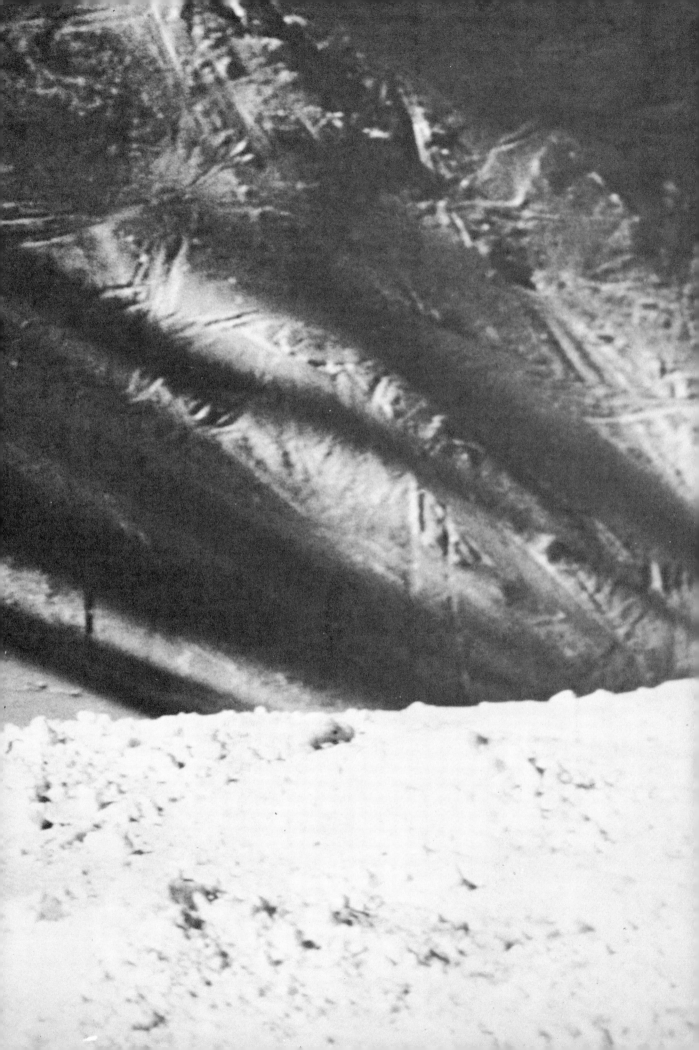

COME RACE WITH ME
3

FIVE ... FOUR ... THREE ... TWO ... ONE ... GO!

DURING MY RACING YEARS, those six words were in a sense, my entire reason for existence. Everything that I had worked for during the week preceding a race—the constant training, the run after run through endless slalom gates, the gymnastics, the increasing tension—all were gathered within me as I waited at the starting gate with the starter's arm on my shoulder.

Twenty-four hours earlier, the tension had begun building up. During the evening before the race, I constantly searched the dial of my wristwatch as if it could make my decisions for me. Should I go to sleep now, or wait for an hour or two? If I went to sleep early, I knew I would lie awake wondering about the following day's outcome. If I waited an hour or two I would be tired enough to sleep, but perhaps too tired in the morning to concentrate on my racing. Another look at my watch and the decision is made: go to bed.

In the morning, I am even more tense. No breakfast; a cold glass of orange juice is all that I can swallow. More decisions. When shall I wax my skis? The base wax had been put on during the previous evening; I will wait until later to put on the mixture that corresponds to my judgement of the weather and snow conditions.

Then, as the examination of the course begins, I am able to divert my mind to the gate combinations until all seems simple and the entire course is clearly outlined in my mind. Finally, the starting gate, and with the starter's hand on my shoulder I suddenly feel too weak to race. There seems to be nothing left of the tremendous power and strength that flowed within me three days earlier during training. Then, *I* was the master of the situation; I controlled my skis and each muscle in my body and knew that I could do everything to perfection.

Now I have doubts about my ability, about the strength in my legs. But suddenly, GO! I am off and two seconds after leaving the gate, the strength is back and the self-confidence has returned and I feel as if no power in the world can stop me from winning.

The farther down the course I get, the more my concentration improves. My body and skis obey my mind; all is harmony and rhythm and I pass through the finish gate knowing I have won.

174

That's the way it was with me and that's the way it is with racers today. There are always doubts and uncertainties. One day everything seems possible. During the next race, however, somewhere the concentration slips for an instant. A mistake is made, the racer is down. In the time it takes to flick an eyelash a championship is won or lost. Sometimes the racer is clumsy; the course has won. No one ever is so good that the course does not get the better of him more than once.

But this, to me, is the charm of competition: to be happy for the winner even though you are angry with yourself for letting the course take you. On those losing days, tired as you are, there is always another race in which you will do better.

All good racers know this. While their feelings during a race usually are the same, their abilities and their styles differ. It would be presumptuous of me to attempt to teach, in a book, the technique one uses in coming down a slalom, or a giant slalom, or a downhill course. I would rather leave teaching to the coaches and instead describe my own experiences in racing, out of which each budding racer may find something he can use for himself.

Let's go back to the 1948 Olympics at St. Moritz where Norway fielded its first alpine team after the Second World War. I was on the team, as was my brother. We were part of a group of twelve top Norwegian skiers who had trained together in the two years following the war's end.

We had no illusions about winning. We had trained on our own without seeing any of the international champions in action. All things considered, we didn't fare too badly in our best event, slalom, in which our best time was 29th.

But in downhill we were laughable. We had no concept of prejumping and it was only our tough physical condition that kept us from crippling ourselves. During the race, I hit one mogul, sailed at least seventy feet through the air and landed in a heap. I had no intension of giving up. I tried another bump that threw me onto the next pitch and down I went. I passed through the finish line looking like a snowman on skis.

After St. Moritz, we returned to Oslo and began intensive training. I knew that I was capable of winning if I put my mind to it; all of the problems at the Olympics had been problems of technique that I felt could be overcome. I had no trouble convincing my parents; they were satisfied to help me with my racing career, as the University was now behind me.

In the fall of 1949 we began training in earnest. We ran every day; we took physical conditioning and gymnastic training twice a week. When the snow came we practiced on the two slalom hills outside of Oslo. As darkness comes early in Norway, most of our training was done under lights. We practiced on hard-packed snow that had the

Stein is congratulated for slalom win at 1954 FIS at Åre. Conditioning paid off.

consistency of marble, on ice—on every conceivable kind of snow except the fresh, powdery kind. Only occasionally that winter was the snow exceptional.

Like a solitary band of recluses we trained, and as we trained, we learned about racing. We learned from each other's mistakes and from our own. We argued, we criticized each other's skiing, and day by day we improved.

Our system of training for slalom was simple. As the hills were low, we set short courses of fifteen to twenty gates. This proved to be very practical; on a long course one has a tendency to forget one's mistakes in the first few gates. On our short courses, which everyone took turns setting, we were able to see every move. After each run we would side step up the course and examine our tracks like medical students dissecting a cadaver. Were we slipping too much? Or turning too late? The tracks showed it. Did we have our weight distributed properly? The tracks showed it; they showed everything.

Before races we would set up longer courses of some fifty to sixty gates on which we would run time trials. The time trials were inevitably exciting. There were times when we felt that it was impossible to go any faster on a certain course and then someone would come in two-tenths of a second faster than everyone else. Immediately we would climb the hill to examine his track and try to understand what he had done to shave his time.

We fell a lot and I think I fell more than anyone else. I always trained by skiing faster and taking more chances than I would during a race—a constant search to find that precise point of balance and just how far I could push myself. I fell during races, too, but in 1949 I found I was standing up more often and also winning more often.

In 1950, the Norwegian team journeyed to Aspen, Colorado, for the World Championships. I had determined that there was much for me to learn about skiing and conditioning and I decided to arrive before the rest of the team. I came to Aspen on December 10, 1949, and immediately began a solitary ordeal that lasted until the rest of the team arrived about a month later.

There is very little that can faze an Aspen citizen, but even to the residents of this Rocky Mountain resort I must have seemed somewhat strange—a young Norwegian of no particular prominence who took sauna baths two or three times a week and ran up and down Ajax (now Aspen) Mountain. This, in fact, is what I did until the snow came. In those days, a miners' train ran halfway up the mountain. I would go with the miners in the early morning, then climb the remainder of the peak. Then I would run down. And I ran through the countryside.

When snow began to accumulate at the top of Ajax I set up my own slalom course on the Buckhorn slope and practiced alone. This had the double purpose of sharpening my reactions, while at the same time I acclimatized myself to the altitude. My life was spartan and it lasted through Christmas, through the New Year. After the rest of the team arrived, I trained with them, and naturally it was more fun to practice as a group. But for myself, I kept to a strict schedule: early nights, no alcoholic drinks, no smoking.

The discipline that I imposed on myself before the Aspen FIS stayed with me through the succeeding years of training for the 1952 Olympics and the 1954 FIS games at Åre. While I did well at Aspen (a bronze in slalom) I know that without such discipline, I would never have done as well as I did later on. Aspen again brought us in contact with the international-class racers. It was a winter of change for me and for other members of our team. We matured that winter. Our technique began to crystallize and our hard physical training began to pay off. We learned confidence in ourselves and in our equipment, and when 1952 rolled around we were ready.

What happened in Oslo in 1952 is outlined in some detail in an earlier chapter. So is the story of the 1954 FIS. That we were successful in our plan of attack is obvious. Therefore, let me tell you some of the things we learned during those bitter years of training and during the later years of success.

TRAINING

IF YOU WANT TO BE A CHAMPION RACER, you must be completely single-minded about maintaining and building your physical condition and stamina. If you expect one hundred percent efficiency out of yourself, you must get adequate sleep every night. Especially important are those crucial nights before races. Don't be tempted by well-meaning friends. They don't have those tough courses to conquer, and you do. You must stick to a regular schedule.

Training itself must be serious—a constant attempt on your part to study and lick those technique problems that are causing you to lose time on a course. But at the same time, there must be some provision for relaxation.

One way to do this is to break up your training sessions with free skiing. Ski all sorts of conditions—ice, hard-pack, powder. Look for the challenging terrain and have fun. Skiing outside of the regular training routine improves your spirit and eliminates that mental staleness that comes from running the same courses day after day.

In Norway, while training for the 1952 Olympics, we would break our training routine for two or three days of free skiing in the mountains. When we came back to our slalom courses, we were eager to go through the gates again. We found that the free skiing had added to our progress. By some subconscious means the technique problems that we had been unable to solve before we left became apparent.

Sometimes we would hang up our alpine skis, and as we were all jumpers, try the jumping hills for an afternoon. On Sundays we often ran cross-country trails for several hours, then we would come home, relax, and wind up the day with a sauna—either at my house or at the Norwegian Ski Museum. Then the following day we'd go back to slalom practice. This was our routine—hard work, relaxation through sauna, healthy food with high vitamin and protein content. Our training was rigorous, but when we raced, it paid off. We felt strong—every muscle in our bodies responded quickly to the demands of the slalom, giant slalom, and downhill courses.

A word of advice to young racers: it is important that your parents be behind you in your racing efforts. You need them to cheer you on, to give you that extra psychological lift on those days during which you do not do so well. I was fortunate to have my family's support—probably because I was determined to finish my education before I assumed a full-time racing career. Both racing and education must meld: to accomplish both is thoroughly satisfying. Besides, the demands of your studies will divert your mind so that when you return to training, you will feel refreshed. The Norwegian and American attitudes toward this are the same, I think. While skiing may be a way of life, it is also important that you finish your college education so that there will be no regrets later.

EQUIPMENT

You must have absolute confidence in your equipment. I have seen young racers "psyched" by the sight of another racer arriving with a half-dozen pairs of skis, or filled with doubt because their combination of waxes is not the one other racers are using.

. During my racing years, I used 7′ 3″ (220 cm.) skis for all events. In the 1954 FIS Games, I raced on *one* pair of skis in all three events.

This may seem strange today when most racers carry at least three pair of skis with them. But I had skied on mine since early in the season and felt so confident on them that I saw no reason to have others. My pair had sixteen holes in each ski. The bindings remained in the same position for giant slalom and downhill. For slalom, I moved them forward about an inch.

The skis had been manufactured by my father's firm. He, my brother and I had designed them. They had multi-grooved bottoms and steel edges and were very flexible with a good camber. Strangely enough, when I examined them after the FIS Games, I found that one ski was warped slightly. I had simply adjusted my skiing to the ski.

Confidence in your equipment has to do with something else that is important to a racer: personal style. You should not follow the lead of a racer who seems to be better than you are. You must find your own solution to your skiing and equipment problems and then, using it as a basis, develop your own method of attack. Champion racers, while they may be aware of the equipment other racers are using, do not let themselves be panicked because the skis, bindings, boots, and poles they themselves use are different.

Another sidelight that helps make the point. My skis had a *double* bottom camber in them. Naturally, they didn't come that way from the factory. I would pair them—put them bottom to bottom with a strap around the tips and the tails. A 2 inch block would be placed about a foot from the tips and another two-inch block would be inserted between the skis about a foot from the tails. Then I would tie a strap around the middle of the skis and place them overnight in our furnace room. In the morning, I immersed them in the snow.

This heating and cooling process produced a rather peculiar looking ski—curved slightly between the tip and the center with another cambered section between the center and the tail. But it worked. When I skied on ice, the skis held better. On softer snow, the skis were still flexible and that kept them from digging in.

The point is simply this: you can win on anything you believe in. I always believed that I was skiing on the best possible equipment for me. I was confident that I was right, and everyone else—wrong.

SLALOM

Slalom is an event that demands utmost concentration, careful planning, and in these days of races lost or won by hundredths of seconds, refined technique.

For the recreational skier, slalom racing is a revelation. A recreational skier viewing his first international slalom race will shake his head with amazement. He will see the best skiers in the world doing exactly the opposite of what he has been taught—weight on the uphill ski, the skis frequently apart, the racers rotate and even snowplow.

This is slalom racing. Style is secondary and time is primary. The top racers have developed their own styles according to their own abilities. There is little in slalom that compares with recreational skiing. The racer is, in a sense, an acrobat. For him the impossible becomes possible.

For instance, easy gate combinations and flat sections of a course can, at times, be skied more effectively with the weight on the uphill ski. Change of weight is time-consuming.

Sometimes a racer can be seen in a skating position when he comes out of a gate. This is because the skating step increases his speed out of the gate and brings him in proper position for the next gate. Had he remained in the turn without skating, valuable time would have been lost by a longer curve. He would have been in an improper position for the next turn.

Snowplowing is commonly used instead of a check or heel thrust when the racer is moving directly downhill. A snowplow check is safe and effective. For example, let us say that the racer is in position for the next gate but is coming in to it too fast. He throws in a quick snowplow check to slow down his speed without changing his line and goes into the gate at a speed he can confidently handle.

When the course is steep, the racer's technique becomes more like the style the recreational skier has been taught. Here it is essential that the weight be on the downhill ski, and the comma position is more frequently seen.

Course Memory

The racer must always have a clear mental picture of what the entire course is like. Not only must he memorize the gate combinations, but before he steps into the starting gate, he must know exactly how to approach each combination.

The correct feeling is to be at the start and sense somehow that you have already run the course. Doing this involves not a trick memory, but the ability to concentrate—to narrow one's mind down to the definite problems of the course to the exclusion of everything else. The racer, as he side steps up the course should not be conscious of the crowd or of other racers. He must firmly establish in his mind the sequence of gates and how he is going to take them.

My own technique consists of studying not only the individual gates, but more importantly, combinations of four and five at a time. As I climb alongside the flags, I decide how to run these groups. Slalom courses are set up in these patterns. The way I run the first gate in a three-gate combination will effect how I come out of the third gate and prepare for the fourth.

Try, then, to put together all of the combinations on the course so that by the time you have climbed to the topmost gate, you have a clear picture in your mind of the whole course.

This should be happening about an hour before the race is to start. If you allow enough time after you have finished studying the course, there is always the opportunity to ski down to that puzzling 47th gate and examine it closely, then close your eyes and put your entire run together again. This will add to your confidence when you step into the starting gate. To be plagued by doubt as you push off will probably mean a lost race.

Racing Strategy

The system that proved successful for me in the 1952 Olympics and the 1954 World Championships was a simple one. In effect I "skied myself in" during the first six or eight slalom gates (first four in giant slalom, first two in downhill). In those gates I found my rhythm and calmed myself down by skiing carefully and relatively slowly. The tenths of seconds I may have lost in those gates were nothing compared to the *seconds* I might have lost had I been forced to struggle through the bottom gates without control and rhythm. I was also able to conserve my strength.

By using this system, you build up your confidence at the top of the mountain. Then you are able to let your skis go. The racer who fights his way down from the very top often loses concentration near the bottom; suddenly he is taking gates too low, his legs are tired, his energy is gone—and so is his hope of placing well.

Here is a typical problem.

After climbing to the start, you find yourself in doubt about a gate combination half-way down the course. If you enter the combination from the left, you know that there is a chance you may not make it, as there is less room in which to maneuver. But while it is chancy, it will definitely cut your time, because it is the shortest route through this particular gate.

You can also take it from the right, in which case you will have more room to maneuver and your rhythm will not be disturbed. But it is the longer way around.

What should you do?

My strategy has always been to consider that there are two runs in slalom. I play it safe in the first run, knowing that the hundredth of a second lost in taking that particular gate from the right can be made up during the second run. But a fall or a disqualification can never be made up. In the second run you have a choice of going for broke or again playing it safe. My rule has been to ski at the same speed, or perhaps a shade faster during the second run and take no chances if I have had a winning time in the first run. But if I am behind after the first run, then I have no alternative but to go all out. The question is asked, "why not play it safe during the second run and settle for fifth or sixth place?" My answer is: settling for fifth or sixth place will never make a champion racer out of anyone.

Some Technique Points

Look Ahead: In running slalom (and this is true for giant slalom as well) always concentrate, not only on the gate you are in, but on the next combination, too. You should always be prepared for the succeeding combinations. If you keep this in mind, you will always be prepared for a misstep. For instance, if I find myself lower in a gate than I should be (causing too wide a turn) I don't wait until the turn is finished and struggle to come up to the next gate. I immediately *skate* into position high enough to give me a straight line through the next combination. Skating in slalom is very effective and can be absolutely necessary in order to maintain the fastest possible line.

Skating step is clearly demonstrated by Stein as he passes through a gate and lines up for the next combination.

189

THE STEP TURN

For hairpins and other gate combinations, instead of checking on each turn, which reduces speed because of heel-thrusting, I place my uphill ski in the direction I want to go and immediately lift my downhill ski next to it. By using this step turn there is no reduction in speed; again I am able to ski the shortest possible line through the gates.

POLE ACTION
Pole action must be quick and rhythmic. One hand and pole is always in front so that your weight is constantly forward. Study the accompanying illustration carefully.

USE OF THE REVERSE SHOULDER
The reverse position allows you to get as close to the slalom poles as possible, which of course shortens your line. By using the reverse shoulder, you are able to edge the inside edge of the downhill ski so that this ski carves in the snow rather than slips.

*In the middle of
a flush combin-
ation, Stein
shows all of the
elements of
good slalom form.*

PRE-RACE ROUTINE:
Countdown to Pushoff

The evening before: Scrape off all of the wax on your skis and put on a new coat of base wax. Check your edges and file them properly. This is especially important if you expect the course to be icy. Proper

In the morning: Eat a light breakfast. For me, milk or sweet tea was always sufficient, because I knew that my coach would always be waiting at the starting gate with my favorite drink—an energy-giving mixture

A half-hour before the start: In slalom events, I always made a point of allowing myself at least a half-hour before the start to get myself ready. I had fixed the course in my mind, was certain about the gate combinations, and now had time to relax for a few moments. I sipped

Ten minutes before the start: Now is the time to relace the boots. If you lace them too early, through the loss of blood circulation in the feet, you will have less control once you are on the course. Put on the skis and check everything again. At this point, I always warmed up

The last few minutes: Review the course and the gate combinations. A cardinal rule that I always forced myself to obey: never watch the first racers go down. I concentrated entirely on thinking about my own race and how I would run it. Watching the racers ahead of you

filing means that the edges must not be over-sharp, and that there must be no burrs or file marks on the edges. A pocket hone, used lightly after filing, will eliminate burrs. Get to sleep early.

of concentrated grape-sugar and water. I drank this a half hour before the start to give me an extra reserve of strength. Wax according to your own experience with snow conditions and temperature.

the grape-sugar drink, checked my bindings, my longthongs, and my ski pole straps. My pole straps were never loose—always tight for more control. One race had been lost for lack of a short strap; I had lost my grip on the pole during a crucial turn.

by making some quick turns near the starting gate—moving around on the skis to get my system going. Never start cold; it will take too long to warm up once you are on the course, and precious time will be lost.

on the course will set up the thought, "I can never go that fast." It will "psych" you and when the starter begins the countdown, you will not be ready. And ready and eager you must be.

GIANT SLALOM

In giant slalom, the racer has only one opportunity to make good. All of his knowledge, experience, and strength must go into the one run through as many as sixty gates. In my experience, there is only one way to ski giant slalom: with great determination but without taking too many chances.

Here is a typical problem I have faced in giant slalom. After studying the course very carefully, I see that there is a difficult combination of gates about halfway down the course. If I take it from the left, because of the terrain variations (a bump) I might be thrown into the air out of control. But taking this chance and succeeding might mean a one-tenth of a second gain in time. Approaching the gate from the right is safe—my skis will stay on the snow. What do I do?

The decision has to be made while I am on the course. In the first few gates everything is going well. I'm taking them exactly as planned —going out of them with more speed than going in. My time is fast as I reach the problem combination. So I go into the gates from the right—playing it safe.

However, if I had skied the first few gates perfectly and then suddenly had caught an edge causing me to lose my rhythm and speed, I would have handled the combination differently. Assuming that I had regained my rhythm before reaching the combination, I would then take it from the left—trying to make up the time I had lost farther up the course.

The point, of course, is that the racer must have the same powers that are necessary in slalom—concentration, strength, quick reactions. But as the giant slalom course is longer, there is more opportunity to correct one's mistakes while on the course.

DOWNHILL

Downhill has never been my favorite event. For me, the chances one had to take to be successful in downhill were not worth the punishment the body would take if a mistake was made. The downhill races I won occurred only when I skied fast, but slowed slightly on the hazards.

Downhill racing takes utmost concentration and utmost fitness. One rule: never enter a downhill race unless you are in perfect physical condition. I once raced in the Holmenkollen downhill with a temperature of 102°. Somewhere on the course I came up to a bump that threw me into the air at least seventy feet. I landed close to the base of a big fir tree. As I picked myself up I realized, with a shudder, that had I flown another few feet, I would have hit the tree. The incident tempered my downhill racing for the remainder of my career. I knew that the bump would have been easy to pre-jump, but my illness had caused me to lose my concentration for a split second, which was enough to end the race for me.

In downhill, as in giant slalom, early preparation in the turns is very important. The racer must make smooth, long turns on as flat a ski as possible. Edging reduces speed by causing friction and has a braking effect.

In planning a downhill run, again as in giant slalom, memory plays an important role. The racer must know where to tuck to attain maximum speed, and where he must pre-jump. In tucking, the weight must be kept slightly back; do not hang forward in the bindings.

The racer must learn to keep in the tuck as he crosses the finish line. Too many races have been lost because the racer stood up before passing through the final gate. Even a slight raising of the upper body out of the tuck will slow the racer down because of air friction.

Still, despite the dangers, downhill racing can be eminently satisfactory, because it gathers inwardly everything one knows about skiing. I can remember downhill races when I felt so steady, it seemed as if I could make my skis do anything I wanted them to do. My skis and legs were one—an extension of myself. They rested against each other; I had the strange feeling that I was cuddling with them and the snow.

Then, as I rushed down the course, I could feel the rhythm, weight, and speed as a harmonious whole. Everything seemed possible. I sped toward a large mogul and my movements were so light and easy that I lifted off the snow and landed with a graceful give in my knees below the mogul—as if it were not there. In the turns I forced the skis into the snow surface so that there was even pressure on them. My body leaned into the hill, controlled perfectly by the fine balance of speed and centrifugal force.

I was unaware of everything outside of the course. Only the terrain ahead interested me. Everything that I knew and had trained for was gathered into these supreme moments of racing.

It did not matter: downhill, giant slalom, or slalom. I loved racing; I raced whether I won or lost. Had it been a duty I would never have raced. But skiing, for me, has never been a duty. It has been my life.

The pride of
accomplishment
that comes
from doing it well...

The challenge:
to reach the absolute
climax of what
is possible for you . . .

INDEX